# THE
# Weeknight Survival Cookbook

## How to Make Healthy Meals in 10 Minutes

### Dena Irwin, R.D.

CHRONIMED PUBLISHING

To my husband Bob, for his ongoing support and encouragement, and to my children Rachel and Daniel, who have changed my life for the better and who have unknowingly been the inspiration for this book.

The Weeknight Survival Cookbook: How to Make
Healthy Meals in 10 Minutes © 1998 by Dena Irwin, R.D.

**Library of Congress Cataloging-in-Publication Data**
Irwin, Dena
The weeknight survival cookbook / by Dena Irwin

         p.          cm.

Includes index.

ISBN 1-56561-165-9;      $14.95

Acquiring Editor: Jeff Braun
Copy Editor: Jolene Steffer
Text Design & Production: David Enyeart
Art/Production Manager: Claire Lewis
Cover Design: Robert Aulicino

Printed in the United States

Published by
Chronimed Publishing
P.O. Box 59032
Minneapolis, MN 55459-0032

10   9   8   7   6   5   4   3   2   1

# Contents

# Introduction

Shopping? Cooking? After a long day at work, who has time to prepare a healthy meal? Well, healthful meals don't have to take a long time to prepare. I am a busy working mom who arrives home from work at 6 p.m. with very hungry children. I don't have the time or energy to spend the evening cooking and cleaning up.

So, what's quick? Most quick cookbooks define quick as 30 minutes. Who has 30 minutes? I think 10 minutes is quick. Once you prepare the head-start meal at the beginning of the week, weeknight meals only take about 10 minutes to prepare. To simplify your life even more, weekly menus and shopping lists are provided for each of the 12 weeks. All you need to do is shop once per week using the shopping list, prepare the head-start meal, and use the menus and recipes to have weeknight meals ready in about 10 minutes. Besides the weeknight recipes, additional recipes are provided because there are times when it's impossible to cook the head-start meal (for example, when it's preferable to spend Sunday at the beach).

So, what's healthy? As a nutritionist I want to provide meals that are not only quick but healthy too. I define healthy as being based on the Food Guide Pyramid. All the meals contain grains, vegetables, and protein. Add a glass of skim milk and a fruit-based dessert and you have all five food groups. You can't get more well balanced than that. The meals are also low in fat, containing no more than 30 percent of calories from fat. Beware however, if you are on a sodium restricted diet, the recipes make no attempt to be low in sodium.

What about taste? In addition to being quick and healthy, the recipes taste delicious. They are family tested and approved. The meals are based on what my family likes to eat. There are some vegetarian meals but no tofu because my family won't eat tofu despite its health benefits. I don't care how healthful a food is, you shouldn't eat it unless it tastes good.

With all that in mind, I set out to write this book. What a challenge! The weeknight recipes emphasize speed (10 minutes), nutrition, and taste. This book is designed for people like me—busy working parents who want to feed their families quick, healthy meals that taste good.

Planning meals for the family is hard work. I've already done the planning for you. Each of the 12 weeks is organized with a menu, shopping list, and recipes for the week. Many of the 10-minute weeknight recipes depend on using leftovers from the Sunday head-start meal. Therefore, I recommend you follow the menu for each week in the order given. You must prepare the head-start meal at the beginning of the week and save the leftovers as directed. I like to do the head-start cooking on Sunday. The head-start meal usually takes about 1 to 1 1/2 hours to prepare. All recipes are made with everyday ingredients you should be able to find at any local supermarket. There is no need to make special trips to gourmet stores.

I like to do the shopping and head-start cooking on different days; I find it is just too much to do it all on the same day. I try to do the shopping on Friday afternoon and avoid the supermarkets on the weekend if at all possible. Weekends are too crowded and it takes forever to shop. Before you go shopping, take a look at the list to make sure you have all the staples and seasonings listed. Then add to the list anything else you need for the week. Keep a running list hanging in a visible spot in the kitchen. When you are running low on something add it to the list so you don't run out. Train your family to do this also. You shouldn't go to the supermarket more than once per week. Who has time?

The recipes are simple to prepare and are very forgiving. They are meant for ordinary cooks just like you. I am not a professional chef. I like to cook foods that are easy, healthy, and taste good. Exact amounts are not necessary for good results. In fact, when I cook, the recipes never come out the same twice. They are always good but just a little different each time. All weeknight recipes yield four "normal-size" servings—not skimpy, but not gigantic either. I don't like it when I make a recipe expecting four servings and only get two.

The Monday to Friday weeknight menus require only a minimum number of pots and pans to help save on cleanup (my husband's favorite part of the system). I like evenings to be for family time and not cleanup time.

Also not required are special equipment and a large kitchen. I live in a townhouse with a rather modest kitchen and not a lot of storage space. See "Kitchen Organization" on page 21 for tips on equipment.

The menus don't include dessert but the "Sweet Endings" section on page 161 will provide you with some very easy and quick dessert ideas. Just don't forget to add those items to your shopping list.

# Week 1

## Sunday
Marinated Chicken Breasts
Roasted Vegetables
White Rice

## Monday
Chicken Caesar Salad
Whole-Grain Bread

## Tuesday
Roasted Vegetable and Cheese Pockets
Tabbouleh Salad

## Wednesday
Tuna Salad Niçoise

## Thursday
Spanish Rice, Beans, and Sausage

## Friday
Mediterranean Couscous

# Week 2

## Sunday
Chili
Corn Bread
Broccoli

## Monday
Chili Stuffed Potato with Cheese
Green Salad

## Tuesday
Corn Chowder
Carrot Salad

## Wednesday
Taco Salad

## Thursday
Szechuan Peanut Noodles with
    Broccoli

## Friday
Veggie Burger and Roasted Red
    Pepper Sandwich
Chick-Pea Salad

# Week 3

## Sunday
Crispy Chicken Breasts
Roasted New Potatoes
Ratatouille

## Monday
Oriental Pork and Vegetable Fried
    Rice

## Tuesday
Crispy Chicken Sandwich
Coleslaw

## Wednesday
Capellini with Ratatouille

### Thursday
Potato and Salmon Salad with Peas

### Friday
Seafood Gumbo with Rice

## Week 4

### Sunday
Meatloaf
Mashed Potatoes
Broccoli

### Monday
Cream of Broccoli Soup
Italian Bread
Green Salad

### Tuesday
Rotelle with Meat Sauce
Green Beans

### Wednesday
Bean Burritos
Corn Salsa

### Thursday
Italian Bread Salad with Smoked
   Turkey

### Friday
Tuna Melt Sandwich
Pepper Salad

## Week 5

### Sunday
Roast Chicken with Gravy
Baked Potatoes
Cranberry Sauce
Butternut Squash

### Monday
Hot Chicken Sandwiches
Mixed Vegetables

### Tuesday
Potato and Asparagus Frittata
French Bread

### Wednesday
Harvest Soup
Cheese Toast

### Thursday
Oriental Chicken Noodle Salad

### Friday
Shrimp Scampi Pizza
Spinach Salad

## Week 6

### Sunday
Roast Beef with Gravy
Mashed Potatoes
Carrots
Broccoli

### Monday
Shepherd's Pie

### Tuesday
Couscous Primavera

### Wednesday
Oriental Beef and Broccoli with
   Noodles

### Thursday
Greek Pizza
Green Salad

### Friday
Smoked Turkey Bagel Sandwich
Cold Beet Borscht

# Week 7

## Sunday
Barbecued Chicken Breasts
Spinach
Barley Pilaf

## Monday
Barbecued Chicken Pizza
Green Salad

## Tuesday
Black Bean Soup
Salad Stuffed Pita

## Wednesday
Barbecued Chicken Sandwich
Coleslaw

## Thursday
Italian Sub Sandwich
Corn Relish

## Friday
Capellini Carbonara with Ham and
    Peas

# Week 8

## Sunday
Spaghetti and Meatballs
Green Beans

## Monday
Meatball Sub Sandwich
Green Bean Vinaigrette

## Tuesday
Minestrone Soup

## Wednesday
Meatball Pizza
Green Salad

## Thursday
Hot Dog on Roll
Baked Beans
Sauerkraut

## Friday
Pan Bagna

# Week 9

## Sunday
Marinated Chicken Breasts
Roasted Vegetables
Potato Casserole

## Monday
Cream of Potato Soup
Broccoli Slaw

## Tuesday
Chicken, Pasta, and Vegetable Salad

## Wednesday
Ham and Cheese Omelet Sandwich
Stewed Tomatoes

## Thursday
Chicken Ranch Roll-Up Sandwich
Dilled Pea Salad

## Friday
Hawaiian Pizza
Green Salad

# Week 10

## Sunday
Roast Turkey Breast with Gravy
Cranberry Sauce
Stuffing
Sweet Potatoes
Green Beans

**Monday**
Turkey Waldorf Salad

**Tuesday**
Turkey Casserole

**Wednesday**
Turkey Reuben Sandwich
Cucumber Salad

**Thursday**
Greek Salad with White Beans
Pita Bread

**Friday**
Capellini with Clam Sauce
Snow Pea Salad

# Week 11

**Sunday**
Marinated Grilled Beef
Brown Rice
Broccoli

**Monday**
Oriental Beef Salad

**Tuesday**
Sweet and Sour Beef and Vegetables
    with Rice

**Wednesday**
Veggie Pizza Pasta

**Thursday**
Antipasto Salad
Italian Bread

**Friday**
Seafood Salad Roll-Up Sandwich
Three-Bean Salad

# Week 12

**Sunday**
Eggplant Parmesan
Garlic Green Beans
Ziti

**Monday**
Eggplant Parmesan Sandwich
Green Bean Vinaigrette

**Tuesday**
Greek Pasta

**Wednesday**
Roast Beef Sandwich with
    Horseradish Sauce
Green Salad

**Thursday**
Egg Drop Soup
Ramen Noodles

**Friday**
Paella Couscous

# The Food Guide Pyramid—Hints for a Healthy Diet

The Food Guide Pyramid is a guideline to follow for healthy eating. There are five major food groups and a "use sparingly" group or what I refer to as the "junk food" group. The pyramid illustrates the importance of eating a variety of foods from all of the five food groups. Try to choose the low-fat foods from within each group. Foods high in fat and sweets should be used sparingly. When I plan menus, I include foods from at least three of the food groups at each meal, and keep added fats to a minimum.

**Fats, Oils & Sweets**
Use sparingly

These symbols show fat
and added sugars in foods:
▼ Fats (naturally occurring
and added)
● Sugars (added)

**Milk, Yogurt & Cheese**
2–3 servings daily

**Meat, Poultry,
Fish, Dry Beans,
Eggs & Nuts**
2–3 servings daily

**Vegetables**
3–5 servings daily

**Fruits**
2–4 servings
daily

**Breads, Cereals, Rice & Pasta**
6–11 servings daily

## What counts as a serving? It's not what you think.

Serving sizes are typically much smaller than people realize, but it's fine to eat more than one serving of a food at a time. For example, a typical pasta portion is 2 to 3 ounces or 1 cup to 1 1/2 cups, which would be 2 to 3 servings from the grain group. Look below to find food groups and serving sizes.

**Grain Group: 6–11 servings daily—The best choices are whole grains**
1 slice or 1 ounce bread
1/2 cup cooked cereal, rice, or pasta
1 ounce ready-to-eat cereal

**Vegetable Group: 3–5 servings daily—The best choices are dark green and deep orange-yellow colored**
1 cup raw vegetables
1/2 cup cooked vegetables
3/4 cup vegetable juice

**Fruit Group: 2–4 servings daily—The best choices are whole fruits or unsweetened canned fruits; select citrus fruits often**
1 medium piece of fruit
1/2 cup canned fruit
3/4 cup fruit juice

**Milk Group: 2–3 servings daily—The best choices are nonfat or low fat**
1 cup milk or yogurt
1 1/2 ounces cheese

**Meat Group: 2–3 servings daily—The best choices are lean cuts of meat, poultry without skin, low-fat selections**
2–3 ounces cooked meat, poultry, or fish
1/2 cup cooked beans, 1 egg, and 2 tablespoons peanut butter all count as
   1 ounce of meat

**Fats, Oils, and Sweets: use sparingly—The best fat choices are unsaturated fats, which are liquid at room temperature, whereas saturated fats are solid at room temperature.**

# Supermarket Survival Guide—Aisle-by-Aisle Tips

The average supermarket contains 40,000 items! Who has time to analyze every product for nutrient content? Here is an aisle-by-aisle guide for quick, nutritious shopping. I keep a very well stocked kitchen. I find that having the right ingredients on hand is key to quick and healthy cooking. This guide is an idea of what my well-stocked kitchen looks like. Sometimes I recommend a fat-free product and sometimes a low-fat product. This is for taste considerations. Some fat-free products taste good but for other products I prefer the low-fat version. Use your own taste when choosing between fat-free and low-fat products.

## Fresh Produce

You've heard it before. Eat five servings a day of fruits and vegetables. They are low in fat and calories, high in fiber, and contain an abundance of vitamins and minerals. It's hard to go wrong in the produce aisle. You won't find nutrition labels on fresh fruits and vegetables, but there should be a sign or poster with nutrient content for the 20 most commonly eaten.

**Best Bets:** Brightly colored vegetables contain antioxidant vitamins that help us stay healthy. Dark green and deep orange-yellow fruits and vegetables are better choices than pale colored produce.

Take advantage of prewashed and precut vegetables. They help save time in the kitchen while fitting in those five-a-day. My local supermarket has a large section devoted to prepared items such as broccoli, cauliflower, carrots, cabbage, squash, and salads. There are also a good variety of prepared fruits like melons and pineapple.

**Beware:** Salad bars are tempting and can be an easy way to quickly serve fruits and vegetables, but avoid items typically made with high-fat ingredients, such as potato salad, pasta salad, antipasto salad, Caesar salad, and coleslaw.

## Canned and Bottled Foods

Canned foods are a great way to save time in the kitchen.

**Best Bets:**

- Tomatoes, tomato sauce, tomato paste, salsa. Stewed tomatoes and garlic-flavored tomatoes are good choices because they are already seasoned.

- Marinara sauce with 3 grams or less fat per serving. Healthy Choice makes excellent sauces that are low in fat.

- Chicken or vegetable broth. I prefer the low-sodium variety.

- Beans or legumes are an excellent way to quickly add protein and great flavor to a meal. They are also low in fat and high in fiber. My favorites are kidney beans, chick-peas, and black beans.

- Canned vegetables can be used as an ingredient when preparing a quick meal. Corn, mushrooms, beets, sliced water chestnuts, and bean sprouts work well.

- Canned fruit packed in fruit juice and applesauce make easy desserts. Cranberry sauce.

- Tuna, sardines, clams, and salmon are all great ways to quickly add seafood to a meal.

- Roasted sweet red peppers are a delicious low-calorie addition to any recipe. I use them in salads, sandwiches, and anyplace where I want to add extra flavor and color.

- Fat-free gravy.

- Evaporated skim milk is good to have on hand to use in place of cream in a recipe.

- Natural-type peanut butter.

- Fat-free salad dressings and mayonnaise are tasty time-savers.

- A small amount of olives in a recipe can provide a large amount of flavor.

- Monounsaturated oils to use in cooking. Olive, canola, and peanut oils are my favorites.

**Beware:**

♦ Stay away from processed foods that may contain a lot of fat, such as cream or alfredo sauce, vegetables in butter sauce, and some soups.

♦ Canned and bottled foods can also have a high sodium content. There are many low-sodium varieties available if that is a concern to you.

## Breads and Grains

What could be better than low-fat, high-fiber foods from the bottom of the Food Guide Pyramid? When I use grain mixes I don't add the fat as directed and the results are fine.

**Best Bets:**

♦ Whole grain breads, bakery quality Italian or French breads, pita bread, bagels, English muffins, Italian pizza shells, and fat-free tortillas are all good choices. I keep them stored in the freezer.

♦ Yolk-free egg noodles and pasta. Two of my favorite pastas are couscous and angel hair or capellini pasta. Couscous cooks in five minutes and capellini cooks in only three minutes. Near East makes wonderful seasoned couscous mixes.

♦ Converted white rice and brown rice. I dislike the flavor of instant rice. I'd rather cook long-grain rice ahead of time than rely on instant rice.

♦ Cracked wheat and bulgur. Near East makes wheat pilaf and tabbouleh mixes.

♦ Pearl barley or Near East barley pilaf mix.

♦ Cereals with less than 5 grams of sugar and more than 5 grams of fiber are ideal. In my house sweetened cereals are considered part of the "junk food" group.

♦ Low-fat crackers, rice cakes, and popcorn are good to have for snacking.

♦ Staples such as whole wheat flour, all-purpose white flour, oats, cornmeal, and bread crumbs are essential to have on hand.

**Beware:**

Steer clear of high-fat bakery items like croissants, muffins, doughnuts, pastries, and scones.

♦ Some pasta and rice mixes can be high in fat, especially alfredo or cheese flavors.

## Frozen Foods

**Best Bets:**
- Frozen vegetables and beans without added sauces. On weekends I like to use fresh vegetables, but for weeknight cooking I depend on frozen varieties. Frozen unsweetened fruits.

- Frozen dinners with less than 10 grams fat. Round out the meal with vegetable juice or salad. Fat-free chicken tenders and fish fillets are good to keep on hand in case of emergency.

- Vegetable burgers are quick to prepare and taste great.

- Breakfast items like low-fat waffles and pancakes are always a hit at my house. I serve with a drizzle of syrup and fruit.

- Dessert items like low-fat frozen yogurt, ice milk, sorbet, and popsicles are good to keep in the freezer.

**Beware:**
- Vegetables in cream or cheese sauces.

- Many frozen processed foods are high in fat. Read labels before purchasing.

## Dairy

**Best Bets:**
- Skim or 1% milk, buttermilk, and yogurt. I use buttermilk in cooking and baking.

- Nonfat cottage and ricotta cheese.

- Low-fat cheese with 5 grams or less fat per serving. I like Sargento Light reduced-fat shredded cheeses. I keep them in the freezer.

- Grated Parmesan or Romano cheese.

- Reduced-fat sour cream and cream cheese.

- Egg whites and egg substitutes. The yolks contain all the fat.

- Light tub margarines have the least amount of artery-clogging saturated fat. My favorite margarine is I Can't Believe It's Not Butter fat-free spray margarine. The fat and calorie content is zero and it tastes good.

*The Weeknight Survival Cookbook*

**Beware:**

♦ Beware of dairy products that aren't skim or low fat. The type of fat in dairy products is the saturated type that can raise cholesterol levels.

## Meats, Poultry, and Seafood

Supermarkets are voluntarily providing nutrition information for meats.

**Best Bets:**

♦ White meat poultry, skin removed before eating. Ground turkey or chicken breast.

♦ All fish. Fish is high in omega 3 fatty acids, which have a protective benefit for the heart. One to two fish meals per week can help prevent heart disease.

♦ Extra lean pork, such as tenderloin.

♦ Leanest cuts of red meat, such as top round, eye of round, and round tip, 95 percent lean ground beef. USDA grade select.

♦ Thin & Trim brand lunch meats.

**Beware:**

♦ Meats can contribute a large amount of fat to the diet. Select meats carefully for the leanest cuts. Keep portions of meat to about 3 ounces per person.

## Seasonings

Who wants to eat bland food? Seasonings add flavor without adding fat and calories.

♦ Vinegars such as balsamic, red wine, rice wine, cider, and fruit-flavored.

♦ Soy sauce, stir-fry sauce, and oyster sauce.

♦ Dijon or grainy-type mustards. Yellow mustard for the kids.

♦ Ketchup, cocktail sauce, chili sauce, barbecue sauce, Worcestershire sauce.

♦ Lime juice and lemon juice.

♦ Horseradish.

◆ Spices. My favorite ones are black pepper, chili powder, cumin, garlic powder, oregano, thyme, basil, dill, paprika, red pepper flakes, cinnamon, nutmeg, ginger, and salt.

# The Nutrition Facts Label—How to Interpret

Almost all foods are required by law to have a Nutrition Facts label. The information on the label makes it easier for you to make informed choices about products. Knowing what to look for allows you to read the label quickly and not spend all day in the supermarket. Below is a sample Nutrition Facts label.

## Nutrition Facts
Serving Size 1 cup (248g)
Servings Per Container 4

**Amount Per Serving**

**Calories** 150     Calories from Fat 35

|  | % Daily Value* |
|---|---|
| **Total Fat** 4g | 6% |
| Saturated Fat 2.5g | 12% |
| **Cholesterol** 20mg | 7% |
| **Sodium** 170mg | 7% |
| **Total Carbohydrate** 17g | 6% |
| Dietary Fiber 0g | 0% |
| Sugars 17g | |
| **Protein** 13g | |

| Vitamin A 4% | • | Vitamin C 6% |
|---|---|---|
| Calcium 40% | • | Iron 0% |

\* Percent Daily Values are based on a 2,000 calorie diet. Your daily values may be higher or lower depending on your calorie needs:

| | Calories: | 2,000 | 2,500 |
|---|---|---|---|
| Total Fat | Less than | 65g | 80g |
| Sat Fat | Less than | 20g | 25g |
| Cholesterol | Less than | 300mg | 300mg |
| Sodium | Less than | 2,400mg | 2,400mg |
| Total Carbohydrate | | 300g | 375g |
| Dietary Fiber | | 25g | 30g |

Calories per gram:
Fat 9   •   Carbohydrate 4   •   Protein 4

**Serving Size:** This is the first thing you should look at on the label. All of the nutrient information is based on one serving. If you are going to eat more than one serving as indicated on the label then you have to adjust the nutrient information. For example, most ice creams indicate one serving to be 1/2 cup (about one scoop). If you are going to eat 1 cup or 1 1/2 cups (2 or 3 scoops) then you have to double or triple the calories, fat, and all other nutrients. It's easy to compare products because similar products have similar serving sizes.

**Nutrient List:** Here is where you find the nutrient information. You can compare different products; for example, one pasta sauce may have 10 grams of fat per serving and another sauce 0 fat. Try to focus not only on the "bad" things in food like fat, but focus also on the good things like fiber.

**% Daily Value:** These are not percentages of the nutrients in the food but rather the percentages of the Daily Value. The Daily Value is found at the bottom of the label and is the same on every label, so after you've looked at it once you can ignore it. The Daily Value are numbers set by the government to help you determine how much of each nutrient you should be eating per day. The only problem is that the Daily Value is based on a reference diet of 2,000 calories. Your own Daily Value may be higher or lower depending on how many calories you eat each day. Most people are confused by the % Daily Value and find it easier just to ignore this section.

# Kitchen Organization—Equipment and Ingredients

An organized kitchen is another key to quick weeknight cooking. If it takes 10 minutes to find a saucepan or an ingredient, how are you going to have the meal ready in 10 minutes? Here are some tips on how I keep my kitchen organized.

## Equipment

**Cutting boards:** I have two plastic cutting boards, a large one and a small one, that can be cleaned in the dishwasher. I keep them out on the counter near the sink where I wash vegetables.

**Sharp knives:** I use a 10-inch chef's knife for most chopping. A small 4-inch paring knife and a serrated bread knife are also useful. I keep the knives out on the counter next to the cutting boards. I have high quality knives made of carbon steel that are easy to keep sharp.

**Pots and pans:** A couple of high quality stainless steel saucepans with copper-sandwiched bottoms are all you need for most weeknight cooking.

I use most frequently a large 2-quart saucepan with a tight-fitting lid. A large skillet is essential—one that is 12 inches wide with an oven-safe handle is preferable. Mine has a nonstick coating to make low-fat cooking and cleanup easier. A large 9 x 13 inch roasting or casserole pan is recommended for roasting meats and poultry, and make-ahead casseroles (see page 153). A stovetop grill pan is not essential but nice to have during cold months when I don't want to use the outdoor grill. I use mine to grill chicken breasts and fish. I keep the pots and pans hanging on a pot rack near the stove. I also keep a colander hanging on the rack for draining pasta.

**Bowls and platters:** large ones for preparing and serving salads in the same dish and saving on cleanup.

**Utensils:** I keep spoons, spatulas, ladles, tongs, and whisks next to the stove for easy reach. Pot holders next to the stove are also helpful. Measuring cups and spoons are kept close by, although I usually just estimate amounts. I like to use a measuring cup with a bottom pour spout to separate fat from broth. I find an instant-read thermometer to be indispensable when cooking meats and poultry. Why guess at doneness when you can easily and quickly check the temperature. Scissors are great to have nearby for quickly opening packages and for cutting pizza. A sharp vegetable peeler is a must.

**Microwave oven:** I find essential for reheating foods, quickly defrosting frozen foods, heating casseroles quickly, melting cheese, and much more. There is no need for special microwave cookware, just make sure your plates and bowls are microwave safe. Glass always works well. Plastic wrap can be used for a cover.

**Other appliances:** There are a couple of appliances that I find helpful but not a necessity. A Crockpot is nice when I want to throw some ingredients together in the morning and have dinner ready when I get home (see Crockpot recipes on page 157). I also have a rotisserie for roasting wonderfully-flavored chickens. It takes no effort to roast a chicken on a Sunday afternoon to have during the week.

## Ingredients
Use the "Supermarket Survival Guide" on page 15 to keep a well-stocked kitchen and then keep your well-stocked kitchen organized. I don't have much storage space but I have developed a system that works well for me.

I keep all canned foods grouped together by tomatoes, vegetables, fruits, and beans. Grains such as rice and pasta are kept together. Seasonings and spices are kept near the stove on a lazy Susan. Oils and vinegars are grouped together, but I keep olive oil in a spray bottle near the stove. The freezer is also well organized with vegetables in one place, meats in another, etc. Once you have an organized kitchen you'll quickly see the benefits in keeping it that way.

# Emergency Take Out Tips—Ideas for Healthiest Choices

There are times when even 10 minutes is too long to prepare a meal. Here are some ideas for the healthiest choices in fast food and take out restaurants:

## Fast Food

◆ Fajita

◆ Roast beef or turkey sandwich with low-fat mayonnaise or mustard

◆ Plain hamburger (no cheese)

◆ Grilled or broiled chicken sandwich

◆ Vegetable roll-up sandwiches

◆ Baked potato

◆ Salad with low-fat dressing

◆ Chicken Caesar salad with low-fat dressing

◆ Low-fat frozen yogurt

◆ Pizza with vegetable toppings and less cheese

◆ Soft taco with less cheese and sour cream

## Chicken

◆ Rotisserie chicken without skin

◆ Steamed vegetables

- Zucchini marinara

- New potatoes

- Rice pilaf

## Chinese
- Steamed Peking ravioli

- Hot & sour or wonton soups

- Stir-fried vegetables with chicken or seafood

- Chop suey or chow mein

- Lo mein with vegetables, chicken, or seafood

- Moo shi with vegetables, chicken, or seafood

- White rice

## Italian
- Salad with low-fat dressing

- Pasta e fagioli or minestrone soup

- Pasta with marinara, seafood, or lemon sauce

- Chicken piccata

- Chicken cacciatore

## Beverages
For beverage choices most places offer low-fat milk or unsweetened iced tea instead of sweetened carbonated drinks.

# Week 1

## Menu

### Sunday
Marinated Chicken Breasts
Roasted Vegetables
White Rice

### Monday
Chicken Caesar Salad
Whole-Grain Bread

### Tuesday
Roasted Vegetable and Cheese Pockets
Tabbouleh Salad

### Wednesday
Tuna Salad Niçoise

### Thursday
Spanish Rice, Beans, and Sausage

### Friday
Mediterranean Couscous

# Week 1

## Staples

Grated Parmesan cheese
Sugar
Dijon or grainy-type mustard
Instant low-sodium vegetable or
  chicken broth
Balsamic vinegar
Extra virgin olive oil
Bottled fat-free Caesar salad dressing
Bottled fat-free Italian salad dressing

### Seasonings

Ground cumin
Chili powder
Crushed thyme
Garlic powder
Salt
Pepper

**The Weeknight Survival Cookbook**

# Week 1

## Fresh Produce

3-ounce package sun-dried tomatoes
(not packed in oil)
1 pound baby carrots
1 red bell pepper
1 large onion
1 bunch asparagus
1 medium zucchini
5 ripe tomatoes
2 pounds red potatoes
10-ounce package ready-to-eat
romaine salad
10-ounce package ready-to-eat
Boston salad

## Canned and Bottled Foods

19-ounce can chick-peas
15-ounce can stewed tomatoes
15-ounce can artichoke hearts
7-ounce jar roasted sweet red peppers
2.25-ounce can sliced black olives
Small jar mild salsa
2 7-ounce cans tuna packed in olive
oil

## Breads and Grains

16-ounce box converted white rice
5.8-ounce box Near East couscous,
roasted garlic & olive oil flavor
5.25-ounce box Near East tabbouleh
wheat salad mix
4-count package pita bread rounds
1/2 pound loaf good quality whole-
grain bread
1 box fat-free croutons

## Frozen Foods

10-ounce package green beans
10-ounce package kernel corn
14-ounce package kidney beans

## Dairy Foods

4 ounces crumbled feta cheese
8 ounces Sargento Light reduced-fat
shredded mozzarella cheese
8 ounces fat-free sour cream

## Meats, Poultry, and Seafood

2 pounds chicken breasts, boned and
skinned (8 halves)
14-ounce package Healthy Choice
low-fat polska kielbasa

# Week 1

## Sunday

Start the rice and potatoes first because they take the longest to cook. If you are cooking the chicken in the broiler then prepare the vegetables first. The vegetables can cool to room temperature while the chicken broils in the oven.

## Marinated Chicken Breasts

Note that the chicken breasts need to marinate several hours in advance of cooking.

1/2 cup vegetable or chicken broth
  (instant is fine)

1 tablespoon extra virgin olive oil

3 tablespoons balsamic vinegar

2 teaspoons Dijon or grainy-type
  mustard

1/2 teaspoon garlic powder or
  1 to 2 minced garlic cloves

2 teaspoons sugar

1 teaspoon crushed thyme

1/4 teaspoon freshly ground
  black pepper

Salt to taste, optional

2 pounds chicken breasts, boned
  and skinned (8 halves)

Place all ingredients except chicken breasts in a jar with a tight-fitting lid and shake well. Rinse chicken breasts and pat dry with paper towels. Place chicken breasts and marinade in a locking plastic bag, making sure the chicken is coated well (using a bag saves on cleanup but a shallow dish covered with plastic wrap works just as well). Marinate the chicken in the refrigerator for several hours, turning occasionally. Prepare the outdoor grill, or preheat the broiler, or use a stovetop grill pan. Grill chicken or place under the broiler for about 10 minutes per side. Cooking time will vary depending on the thickness of the chicken. The chicken is done when the internal temperature reaches 165° (use an instant-read thermometer). Discard the marinade.

Makes 8 servings, save half for Monday
Per serving: 164 calories, 25g protein, 3g carbohydrate, 5g fat,
69mg cholesterol, 159mg sodium
Exchanges: 3 meat

# Roasted Vegetables

The vegetables listed here work great but feel free to use whatever vegetables you prefer. Any combination of vegetables will work. Roasting brings out the natural sweetness of vegetables and creates a delicious flavor.

1 red bell pepper, cored and cut into strips

1 bunch asparagus, broken into 1-inch pieces, ends discarded

1 medium zucchini, halved, and cut into 1-inch chunks

1 pound baby carrots

1 teaspoon extra virgin olive oil

Salt to taste, optional

Freshly ground black pepper to taste

Balsamic vinegar to taste

Preheat the oven to 450°. Line two shallow baking pans or cookie sheets with foil (makes cleanup easier). Spread the vegetables in a single layer on the foil-lined sheets. Don't overcrowd or the vegetables will steam instead of roast. You may need to roast the vegetables in two batches. Sprinkle the vegetables with the olive oil or spray with olive oil if you keep your oil in a spray bottle. Roast in the oven for 10 to 15 minutes, stirring once. Transfer the vegetables to a serving bowl and toss with salt, pepper, and vinegar. The vegetables can be served hot, cold, or at room temperature.

**Makes 8 servings, save half for Tuesday**
**Per serving: 50 calories, 2g protein, 10g carbohydrate, 1g fat,**
**0 cholesterol, 51mg sodium**
**Exchanges: 2 vegetable**

# White Rice

16-ounce box converted white rice     4 3/4 cups water

Place the rice and water in a large saucepan. Bring to a boil, cover, and simmer over low heat until the rice is tender and the water is absorbed, about 20 to 25 minutes.

**Makes 8 servings, save half for Thursday**
**Per serving: 205 calories, 4g protein, 45g carbohydrate, 0 fat,**
**0 cholesterol, 2mg sodium**
**Exchanges: 3 starch**

# Red Potatoes

2 pounds red potatoes

Scrub the potatoes. Boil in water to cover until tender or until easily pierced with a fork, about 20 to 25 minutes. Drain and cool. Save for Wednesday.

# Tabbouleh Salad

5.25-ounce box Near East tabbouleh wheat salad mix

Prepare according to package directions, omitting the oil. Save for Tuesday.

## Monday

# Chicken Caesar Salad

10-ounce package ready-to-eat romaine salad

2 ripe tomatoes, quartered

3/4 cup fat-free croutons

2 tablespoons grated Parmesan cheese

1/2 cup bottled fat-free Caesar salad dressing

1/2 recipe marinated chicken breasts, saved from Sunday, sliced

Toss all ingredients together in a large serving bowl.

Makes 4 servings
Per serving: 238 calories, 29g protein, 14g carbohydrate, 6g fat,
71mg cholesterol, 660mg sodium
Exchanges: 3 meat, 1 vegetable, 1 fat

# Whole-Grain Bread

1/2 pound loaf whole-grain bread

Makes 4 servings
Per serving: 106 calories, 7g protein, 25g carbohydrate, 1g fat,
0 cholesterol, 109mg sodium
Exchanges: 2 starch

# Roasted Vegetable and Cheese Pockets

4 large pita bread rounds
8-ounce package Sargento Light
  reduced-fat shredded mozzarella
  cheese

1/2 recipe roasted vegetables, saved
  from Sunday

Cut each pita in half. Stuff pitas equally with cheese and vegetables. Microwave on high for 1 to 2 minutes until cheese is melted and vegetables are heated through.

Makes 4 servings
Per serving: 324 calories, 27g protein, 43g carbohydrate, 6g fat,
16mg cholesterol, 384mg sodium
Exchanges: 2 meat, 2 starch, 1 vegetable

# Tabbouleh Salad

Serve Pockets with tabbouleh salad, saved from Sunday.

Makes 4 servings
Per serving: 100 calories, 4g protein, 26g carbohydrate, 0 fat,
0 cholesterol, 325mg sodium
Exchanges: 1 1/2 starch

# Tuna Salad Niçoise

This classic salad is usually beautifully arranged and presented.
This version is much easier to prepare and tastes just as good.

Cooked red potatoes, saved from
   Sunday, quartered

2 ripe tomatoes, quartered

10-ounce package ready-to-eat
   Boston salad

10-ounce package frozen green
   beans, thawed in the microwave

2 7-ounce cans tuna packed in
   olive oil, drained

1 tablespoon capers

1/2 cup bottled fat-free Italian
   salad dressing

Toss all ingredients together in a large serving bowl.

**Makes 4 servings**
**Per serving: 463 calories, 36g protein, 61g carbohydrate, 9g fat,**
**18mg cholesterol, 821mg sodium**
**Exchanges: 4 meat, 2 starch, 2 vegetable**

# Spanish Rice, Beans, and Sausage

1/2 recipe white rice, saved from
  Sunday

15-ounce can stewed tomatoes

14-ounce package frozen kidney
  beans

10-ounce package frozen kernel
  corn

Half of a 14-ounce package
  Healthy Choice low-fat polska
  kielbasa, sliced 1/4-inch thick

1 tablespoon chili powder

1/2 teaspoon ground cumin

1/2 teaspoon garlic powder

Freshly ground black pepper to taste

Small jar mild salsa, optional

Fat-free sour cream, optional

Combine all ingredients except salsa and sour cream in a large saucepan.
Cook over medium-high heat until heated through, about 5 minutes. Top
each serving with salsa and sour cream if desired.

**Makes 4 servings**
Per serving: 477 calories, 22g protein, 91g carbohydrate, 3g fat,
23mg cholesterol, 551mg sodium
Exchanges: 3 meat, 4 starch, 1 1/2 vegetable

# Mediterranean Couscous

5.8-ounce box Near East couscous, roasted garlic & olive oil flavor

Half of a 3-ounce package sun-dried tomatoes

4 ounces crumbled feta cheese

7-ounce jar roasted sweet red peppers, drained and chopped

15-ounce can artichoke hearts, drained and chopped

15-ounce can chick-peas, drained

2.25-ounce can sliced black olives, drained

1 teaspoon extra virgin olive oil

3 tablespoons balsamic vinegar

Boil water as directed on couscous package. Place couscous, seasoning packet, and sun-dried tomatoes in a large serving bowl. Pour boiling water over couscous and tomatoes, cover bowl with plastic wrap, and let stand for 5 minutes. Fluff couscous with a fork. Add remaining ingredients and mix well.

**Makes 4 servings**
Per serving: 476 calories, 18g protein, 77g carbohydrate, 9g fat, 25mg cholesterol, 1082mg sodium
Exchanges: 1 meat, 3 starch, 3 vegetable, 1 fat

# Week 2

## Sunday
Chili
Corn Bread
Broccoli

## Monday
Chili Stuffed Potato with Cheese
Green Salad

## Tuesday
Corn Chowder
Carrot Salad

## Wednesday
Taco Salad

## Thursday
Szechuan Peanut Noodles with
    Broccoli

## Friday
Veggie Burger and Roasted Red
    Pepper Sandwich
Chick-Pea Salad

# Week 2

## Staples

Raisins
Red wine vinegar
Rice vinegar
Fat-free mayonnaise
Bottled fat-free Italian salad dressing
Sugar
Flour
Baking powder
Baking soda
Cornmeal
Canola oil
Extra virgin olive oil
Vegetable oil cooking spray
Soy sauce
Peanut butter

**Seasonings**
Chili powder
Ground cumin
Crushed thyme
Crushed oregano
Garlic powder
Red pepper flakes
Salt
Black pepper

# Week 2

**Fresh Produce**

2 large onions

2 green bell peppers

2 ripe tomatoes

2 10-ounce packages ready-to-eat
   green salad

1 ripe avocado

6 large baking potatoes (russet)

10-ounce package shredded carrots

2 1/4 pounds broccoli

1 bunch green onions (scallions)

**Canned and Bottled Foods**

2 28-ounce cans crushed tomatoes

2 6-ounce cans tomato paste

19-ounce can chick-peas

15-ounce can kernel corn

16-ounce can cream-style corn

15-ounce can reduced-sodium
   chicken broth

7-ounce jar roasted sweet red peppers

2.25-ounce can sliced black olives

Small jar taco sauce

8-ounce can evaporated skim milk

**Breads and Grains**

4-count package sandwich rolls

8-count package fat-free tortillas

12-ounce package angel hair pasta

**Frozen Foods**

12.8-ounce package Green Giant
   Harvest Burgers

Small package diced onion

Small package diced green bell pepper

2 14-ounce packages kidney beans

16-ounce package kernel corn

**Dairy Foods**

8 ounces fat-free sour cream

8-ounce package Sargento Light
   reduced-fat Mexican shredded
   cheese

Nonfat buttermilk

Eggs

**Meats, Poultry, and Seafood**

2 pounds ground turkey breast or
   95% lean ground beef

4 ounces lean ham steak

# Week 2

To save time and energy put the corn bread and potatoes in the oven at the same time. Simmer the chili and prepare the broccoli while the corn bread and potatoes are baking.

## Chili

For my family I keep this mild by using only 2 tablespoons of chili powder. Adults can add red pepper flakes at the table to spice it up if needed.

| | |
|---|---|
| 1 teaspoon olive oil | 2 6-ounce cans tomato paste |
| 2 large onions, peeled and chopped | 2 to 4 tablespoons chili powder |
| 2 green bell peppers, cored and chopped | 2 teaspoons ground cumin |
| | 2 teaspoons crushed oregano |
| 2 pounds ground turkey breast or 95% lean ground beef | 1 teaspoon garlic powder |
| | Salt to taste, optional |
| 2 28-ounce cans crushed tomatoes | Black pepper to taste |
| 2 14-ounce packages frozen kidney beans | 2 tablespoons red wine vinegar |

In a large pot, sauté the vegetables in olive oil over medium-high heat for a few minutes to soften. Add the turkey or ground beef and continue cooking over medium-high heat for about 10 minutes or until done. If using beef, remove extra fat by draining in a colander and then return to the pot. Add remaining ingredients, bring to a boil, and then reduce heat to low. Simmer uncovered for 30 to 40 minutes until thickened.

Makes 12 servings, save one-third for Monday and one-third for Wednesday
Per serving: 251 calories, 26g protein, 30g carbohydrate, 3g fat,
46mg cholesterol, 443mg sodium
Exchanges: 2 meat, 1 starch, 2 vegetable

# Corn Bread

On the rare occasion when I have leftover corn bread,
I freeze it for making corn bread stuffing at a later time.

Vegetable oil cooking spray

1 cup yellow cornmeal

1 cup all-purpose flour

2 teaspoons baking powder

1/2 teaspoon baking soda

1/2 teaspoon salt

1/3 cup sugar

3 tablespoons canola oil

1 1/4 cups nonfat buttermilk

1 egg

Preheat the oven to 425°. Spray an 8-inch square baking pan with vegetable oil spray. In a large bowl mix together the cornmeal, flour, baking powder, baking soda, salt, and sugar. In a small bowl or measuring cup whisk together the oil, buttermilk, and egg. Add the wet ingredients to the dry ingredients and mix until just combined. Pour the batter into the prepared pan. Bake for 20 minutes or until a toothpick inserted in the center comes out clean.

**Makes 8 servings**
**Per serving: 217 calories, 5g protein, 35g carbohydrate, 7g fat,**
**28mg cholesterol, 373mg sodium**
**Exchanges: 2 starch, 1 fat**

# Broccoli

2 1/4 pounds fresh broccoli

Prepare the broccoli by washing and then cut into small florets. The stems can be peeled and sliced. Place florets and stems in a microwave safe bowl, cover, and microwave on high for 4 to 5 minutes. The broccoli should be tender but not mushy.

**Makes 8 servings, save half for Thursday**
**Per serving: 25 calories, 3g protein, 5g carbohydrate, 0 fat,**
**0 cholesterol, 23mg sodium**
**Exchanges: 1 vegetable**

# Baked Potatoes

6 large baking potatoes (russet)

Preheat the oven to 425°. Wash and scrub the potatoes. Pierce the potatoes several times with a fork. Bake directly on the oven rack for 45 to 60 minutes. The potatoes are done when they can easily be pierced with a fork.

**Makes 6 servings, save 4 for Monday, and save 2 for Tuesday**

## Monday

# Chili Stuffed Potatoes

1/3 recipe chili, saved from
  Sunday

4 baked potatoes, saved from
  Sunday

Half of an 8-ounce package Sargento
  Light reduced-fat Mexican
  shredded cheese

Place the potatoes on a microwave-safe plate and split in half lengthwise. Divide the chili equally onto each of the four potatoes. Top each potato with 1 ounce of cheese. Cover with plastic wrap and microwave on high for several minutes or until heated through and the cheese is melted.

**Makes 4 servings**
**Per serving: 542 calories, 38g protein, 82g carbohydrate, 6g fat,**
**56mg cholesterol, 601mg sodium**
**Exchanges: 3 meat, 3 starch, 2 vegetable**

# Green Salad

10-ounce package ready-to-eat
  green salad

1/2 cup bottled fat-free salad
  dressing

Toss together in a large serving bowl.

**Makes 4 servings**
**Per serving: 21 calories, 1g protein, 4g carbohydrate, 0 fat,**
**0 cholesterol, 296mg sodium**
**Exchanges: 1 vegetable**

## Tuesday

Prepare the carrot salad while the chowder is simmering.

# Corn Chowder

2 baked potatoes, saved from
    Sunday, diced
16-ounce package frozen kernel
    corn
16-ounce can cream-style corn
15-ounce can reduced-sodium
    chicken broth
4 ounces lean ham steak, diced
1/2 cup frozen diced onion
1/2 cup frozen diced green bell
    pepper
1/4 teaspoon crushed thyme
Freshly ground black pepper to taste
1 cup evaporated skim milk

Combine all ingredients in a large saucepan and bring to a boil. Simmer
for a few minutes until heated through.

**Makes 4 servings**
**Per serving: 378 calories, 19g protein, 78g carbohydrate, 2g fat,**
**16mg cholesterol, 634mg sodium**
**Exchanges: 1 meat, 3 starch, 1 vegetable**

# Carrot Salad

This salad can also be made ahead of time.

10-ounce package shredded carrots
3/4 cup raisins
1/2 cup bottled fat-free Italian
    salad dressing

Combine all ingredients together in a large serving bowl.

**Makes 4 servings**
**Per serving: 142 calories, 2g protein, 36g carbohydrate, 0 fat,**
**0 cholesterol, 388mg sodium**
**Exchanges: 1 1/2 vegetable, 2 fruit**

# Taco Salad

8 fat-free tortillas

1/3 recipe chili, saved from Sunday

10-ounce package ready-to-eat
green salad

2 ripe tomatoes, chopped

1 bunch green onions, chopped

2.25-ounce can sliced black olives,
drained

Small jar mild taco sauce

Fat-free sour cream, optional

1 ripe avocado, peeled and sliced,
optional

Using four microwave safe plates, place 2 tortillas on each plate. Divide
the chili equally over the tortillas. Cover the plates with plastic wrap and
microwave on high for about 2 minutes or until heated through. Divide
the salad greens, vegetables, and olives over the warm tortillas and chili.
Top each with 2 tablespoons of taco sauce. Top with sour cream and avocado if desired.

**Makes 4 servings**
**Per serving: 419 calories, 31g protein, 62g carbohydrate, 5g fat,**
**46mg cholesterol, 1000mg sodium**
**Exchanges: 2 meat, 3 starch, 3 vegetable, 1 fat**

# Szechuan Peanut Noodles with Broccoli

I usually omit the red pepper flakes and have adults add their own at the table.

12 ounces angel hair pasta

3 tablespoons peanut butter

4 tablespoons hot water

1 tablespoon soy sauce

2 teaspoons rice vinegar

1 teaspoon sugar

1/8 teaspoon garlic powder

1/4 teaspoon red pepper flakes

1/2 recipe cooked broccoli, saved
   from Sunday

In a large saucepan cook the pasta in 2 quarts of boiling water for 3 minutes. While the pasta is cooking stir together the remaining ingredients except broccoli in a small bowl. You may need to stir for a few minutes until the mixture is smooth. Place the broccoli in a colander. Drain the pasta in the colander directly over the broccoli to heat up the broccoli. Return the drained pasta and broccoli to the pan or serving bowl. Add the peanut sauce and mix well to combine.

**Makes 4 servings**
**Per serving: 418 calories, 16g protein, 72g carbohydrate, 8g fat,**
**0 cholesterol, 362mg sodium**
**Exchanges: 1 meat, 3 starch, 1 vegetable, 1 fat**

# Veggie Burger and Roasted Red Pepper Sandwich

Vegetable burgers have a great taste; just don't expect them to taste like hamburgers. The peppers add moistness as well as flavor.

4 Green Giant Harvest Burgers

4 sandwich rolls

7-ounce jar roasted sweet red peppers

Cook the vegetable burgers in the microwave according to package directions. Place each burger on a roll with a roasted pepper.

**Makes 4 servings**
**Per serving: 243 calories, 8g protein, 43g carbohydrate, 5g fat,**
**0 cholesterol, 533mg sodium**
**Exchanges: 1 meat, 2 starch, 1 vegetable**

# Chick-Pea Salad

19-ounce can chick-peas, drained

1/3 cup fat-free Italian salad dressing

Combine the chick-peas with the salad dressing in a small serving bowl.

**Makes 4 servings**
**Per serving: 150 calories, 6g protein, 28g carbohydrate, 1g fat,**
**0 cholesterol, 550mg sodium**
**Exchanges: 1 starch**

# Week 3

### Sunday
Crispy Chicken Breasts
Roasted New Potatoes
Ratatouille

### Monday
Oriental Pork and Vegetable Fried
   Rice

### Tuesday
Crispy Chicken Sandwich
Coleslaw

### Wednesday
Capellini with Ratatouille

### Thursday
Potato and Salmon Salad with Peas

### Friday
Seafood Gumbo with Rice

# Week 3

## Staples

Lemon juice
Reduced-sodium chicken broth
   (instant is fine)
Fat-free mayonnaise
All-purpose white flour
Peanut oil
Olive oil
Grated Parmesan cheese

### Seasonings
Garlic powder
Crushed oregano
Crushed thyme
Dried basil
Paprika
Dried dillweed
Salt
Black pepper
Hot sauce

# Week 3

**Fresh Produce**

8 medium new potatoes
10-ounce package coleslaw mix
   (shredded cabbage)
2 small eggplant
2 medium zucchini
1 large onion
1 green bell pepper
1 red bell pepper
10-ounce package ready-to-eat salad
2 ripe tomatoes

**Canned and Bottled Foods**

8-ounce can cranberry sauce
15-ounce can salmon
2 15-ounce cans stewed tomatoes
28-ounce can crushed tomatoes
4-ounce can sliced mushrooms
Stir-fry sauce
Bottled fat-free coleslaw dressing

**Breads and Grains**

16-ounce box converted white rice
Cornflake crumbs
4-count package sandwich rolls
12-ounce package angel hair pasta

**Frozen Foods**

16-ounce package peas
16-ounce package sliced okra
16-ounce package mixed stir-fry
   vegetables
14-ounce package white beans

**Dairy Foods**

Eggs
Nonfat buttermilk

**Meats, Poultry, and Seafood**

2 pounds chicken breasts, boned and
   skinned (8 halves)
6 ounces lean ham
1 pound cooked and peeled shrimp or
   imitation seafood

# Week 3

## Sunday

The chicken and potatoes can cook in the oven at the same time. Start the potatoes first since they take longer to cook. The ratatouille and rice can simmer while the chicken and potatoes cook.

## Crispy Chicken Breasts

Kids love this healthier version of chicken nuggets.

1 teaspoon olive oil

2 pounds boned and skinned chicken breasts (8 halves)

1 cup nonfat buttermilk

1 1/2 cups cornflake crumbs

Preheat the oven to 400°. Line a large baking pan with foil (for easy cleanup). Spray or lightly brush the bottom of the pan with half the oil. Rinse chicken breasts and pat dry with paper towels. Put the buttermilk in a shallow bowl or pie plate, and put cornflake crumbs in another. Dip each piece of chicken first in the buttermilk then in the cornflake crumbs. Place the coated chicken into the prepared baking pan. Lightly spray or drizzle the remaining oil on top of the chicken breasts (this makes it crispy). Bake the chicken in the preheated oven for about 45 minutes or until the internal temperature of the chicken reaches 165°.

**Makes 8 servings, save half for Tuesday**
**Per serving: 166 calories, 19g protein, 15g carbohydrate, 3g fat,**
**47mg cholesterol, 252mg sodium**
**Exchanges: 2 meat, 1/2 starch**

# Roasted New Potatoes

I like these potatoes plain but seasonings such as rosemary and garlic are nice additions.

8 medium red potatoes

2 teaspoons olive oil

Salt to taste

Freshly ground black pepper to taste

Preheat the oven to 400°. Scrub but do not peel the potatoes. Cut the potatoes into 1-inch pieces. Place the potatoes in a large baking pan and toss with the oil and seasonings. Bake the potatoes in the preheated oven, stirring once or twice, for about an hour or until a fork easily pierces the potatoes.

**Makes 8 servings, save half for Thursday**
**Per serving: 195 calories, 3g protein, 43g carbohydrate, 1g fat,**
**0 cholesterol, 14mg sodium**
**Exchanges: 2 starch**


# Ratatouille

1 teaspoon olive oil

1 large onion, peeled and chopped into 1/2-inch pieces

2 small eggplant, unpeeled and chopped into 1/2-inch cubes

2 medium zucchini, chopped into 1/2-inch cubes

1 green bell pepper, cored and chopped into 1/2-inch pieces

1 red bell pepper, cored and chopped into 1/2-inch pieces

4-ounce can mushrooms, drained

28-ounce can crushed tomatoes

1/2 teaspoon garlic powder

1/2 teaspoon crushed thyme

1/2 teaspoon crushed oregano

1/2 teaspoon dried basil

1/4 teaspoon freshly ground black pepper

In a large nonstick skillet, sauté the onion, eggplant, zucchini, and peppers in the oil over medium-high heat for about 10 minutes or until the vegetables are tender but not mushy. Add the remaining ingredients, bring to a boil, reduce heat, and simmer uncovered for about 10 minutes.

**Makes 8 servings, save half for Wednesday**
**Per serving: 71 calories, 3g protein, 14g carbohydrate, 1g fat,**
**0 cholesterol, 308mg sodium**
**Exchanges: 3 vegetable**

# White Rice

16-ounce box converted white rice    4 3/4 cups water

Place the rice and water in a large saucepan. Bring to a boil, cover, and simmer over low heat until the rice is tender and the water is absorbed, about 20 to 25 minutes.

**Makes 8 servings, save half for Monday and half for Friday**

## Monday

# Oriental Pork and Vegetable Fried Rice

Fried rice should always be made with cold rice. If warm rice is used, it sticks and becomes mushy. Any combination of leftover cooked meats, poultry, seafood, and vegetables works well.

1 egg

1 teaspoon peanut oil

1/2 recipe cooked white rice, saved from Sunday

16-ounce package frozen mixed stir-fry vegetables

6 ounces lean ham, cut into small pieces

1/2 cup stir-fry sauce

In a large nonstick skillet, scramble the egg and then remove from the pan and set aside. Add the oil and rice to the pan and stir-fry the rice over high heat for a few minutes until the rice starts to brown. Add the vegetables, cover, and cook for about 5 minutes. Add the scrambled egg, chopped ham, and stir-fry sauce to the rice and vegetables and mix to combine.

**Makes 4 servings**
**Per serving: 310 calories, 19g protein, 49g carbohydrate, 4g fat,**
**73mg cholesterol, 1450mg sodium**
**Exchanges: 2 meat, 2 starch, 3 vegetable**

# Crispy Chicken Sandwich

1/2 recipe crispy chicken breasts,
   saved from Sunday (4 halves)
4 sandwich rolls

8-ounce can cranberry sauce
Fat-free mayonnaise, optional

Heat the chicken in the microwave on high for a few minutes or until heated through. Place each chicken breast half on a sandwich roll; add cranberry sauce. Top with mayonnaise if desired.

**Makes 4 servings**
**Per serving: 364 calories, 23g protein, 56g carbohydrate, 5g fat,**
**47mg cholesterol, 504mg sodium**
**Exchanges: 2 meat, 2 1/2 starch**

# Coleslaw

This can also be made ahead of time but is just as good when first made.

10-ounce package coleslaw mix (shredded cabbage)
1/2 cup bottled fat-free coleslaw dressing
Freshly ground black pepper to taste

In a large serving bowl, combine the cabbage and dressing until mixed well. Season with black pepper.

**Makes 4 servings**
**Per serving: 40 calories, 1g protein, 8g carbohydrate, 0 fat,**
**0 cholesterol, 224mg sodium**
**Exchanges: 1 1/2 vegetable**

## Capellini with Ratatouille

12 ounces capellini (angel hair pasta)

1/2 recipe ratatouille, saved from Sunday

Half of a 14-ounce package frozen white beans

Grated Parmesan cheese, optional

Cook pasta in 2 quarts of boiling water for 2 to 3 minutes. While the pasta is cooking, heat the ratatouille and beans together in a large saucepan. Drain the pasta and toss with the ratatouille and bean mixture. Serve with Parmesan cheese if desired.

Makes 4 servings
Per serving: 451 calories, 18g protein, 89g carbohydrate, 2g fat,
0 cholesterol, 315mg sodium
Exchanges: 1 meat, 5 starch, 3 vegetable

## Potato and Salmon Salad with Peas

16-ounce package frozen peas

1/2 recipe roasted new potatoes, saved from Sunday

15-ounce can salmon, drained

1/2 cup fat-free mayonnaise

1 tablespoon lemon juice

1 teaspoon dried dillweed

Freshly ground black pepper, to taste

10-ounce package ready-to-eat salad

2 ripe tomatoes, sliced

Defrost the peas in the microwave. In a large serving bowl, combine the peas, potatoes, salmon, mayonnaise, lemon juice, dill, and pepper. Serve the salad over lettuce and tomato.

Makes 4 servings
Per serving: 477 calories, 33g protein, 68g carbohydrate, 8g fat,
59mg cholesterol, 925mg sodium
Exchanges: 2 meat, 3 1/2 starch, 1 vegetable

# Seafood Gumbo with Rice

2 15-ounce cans stewed tomatoes

16-ounce package frozen sliced okra

1 pound cooked shrimp or
  imitation seafood

1 cup reduced-sodium chicken
  broth (instant is fine)

1 teaspoon garlic powder

1 teaspoon crushed thyme

1 teaspoon paprika

Few drops hot sauce, optional

2 tablespoons all-purpose flour

1/4 cup water

1/2 recipe cooked white rice, saved
  from Sunday

In a large saucepan, combine the tomatoes, okra, seafood, broth, garlic, thyme, paprika, and hot sauce. Bring to a boil, reduce heat, and simmer for a few minutes until the okra is heated through. Combine the flour and water in a jar and shake well. Add the flour mixture to the saucepan and continue to cook for a minute until the mixture thickens. While the gumbo is simmering, reheat the rice in the microwave. Serve the gumbo over rice.

**Makes 4 servings**
**Per serving: 316 calories, 22g protein, 55g carbohydrate, 1g fat,**
**0 cholesterol, 1004mg sodium**
**Exchanges: 2 meat, 2 starch, 4 vegetable**

# Week 4

### Sunday
Meatloaf
Mashed Potatoes
Broccoli

### Monday
Cream of Broccoli Soup
Italian Bread
Green Salad

### Tuesday
Rotelle with Meat Sauce
Green Beans

### Wednesday
Bean Burritos
Corn Salsa

### Thursday
Italian Bread Salad with Smoked
    Turkey

### Friday
Tuna Melt Sandwich
Pepper Salad

# Week 4

## Staples

Fat-free mayonnaise
Bottled fat-free Italian salad dressing
Worcestershire sauce
Ketchup
Grated Parmesan cheese

**Seasonings**
Garlic powder
Salt
Black pepper

# Week 4

## Shopping List

### Fresh Produce
3 pounds Yukon Gold potatoes
2 1/4 pounds broccoli
10-ounce package ready-to-eat green salad
10-ounce package ready-to-eat Italian blend salad
4 ripe tomatoes
1 medium cucumber
1 red onion
1 green bell pepper

### Canned and Bottled Foods
26-ounce jar Healthy Choice pasta sauce
16-ounce can fat-free refried beans
16-ounce jar picante sauce
16-ounce jar salsa
2 7-ounce cans tuna packed in olive oil
Small bottle capers
Small bottle pitted kalamata or Greek-style olives
15-ounce can reduced-sodium chicken broth

### Breads and Grains
1 pound loaf good quality Italian bread
4-count package sandwich rolls
8-count package fat-free tortillas
12-ounce package rotelle pasta
Toasted bread crumbs

### Frozen Foods
16-ounce package Italian-style green beans
16-ounce package mixed pepper strips
16-ounce package kernel corn

### Dairy Foods
Skim milk
4-ounce carton egg substitute
8-ounce package Sargento Light reduced-fat shredded cheddar cheese
8-ounce package Sargento Light reduced-fat shredded mozzarella cheese
8-ounce container fat-free sour cream

### Meats, Poultry, and Seafood
2 pounds ground turkey breast or 95% lean ground beef
8 ounces smoked turkey breast

# Week 4

Prepare the potatoes and broccoli while the meatloaf cooks.

## Meatloaf

2 pounds ground turkey breast or
  95% lean ground beef
1 cup toasted bread crumbs
1/2 cup egg substitute
1/2 cup warm water
1/2 cup ketchup, divided

2 teaspoons Worcestershire sauce
1/8 teaspoon freshly ground black
  pepper
1/2 teaspoon garlic powder
1 green bell pepper, cored and sliced

Preheat the oven to 350°. In a large bowl, combine the turkey breast or ground beef, bread crumbs, egg substitute, water, 1/4 cup of ketchup, Worcestershire sauce, black pepper, and garlic powder. Pat the meat mixture into an 8 x 4 inch baking pan. Top with remaining 1/4 cup ketchup and sliced peppers. Bake for about 1 hour and 15 minutes.

**Makes 8 servings, save half for Tuesday**
**Per serving: 226 calories, 29g protein, 14g carbohydrate, 5g fat,**
**69mg cholesterol, 314mg sodium**
**Exchanges: 3 meat, 1/2 starch, 1 fat**

## Mashed Potatoes

Yukon Gold potatoes have such a buttery taste and texture that no added fat is needed. You can easily make these into garlic mashed potatoes by boiling 6 peeled garlic cloves with the potatoes and mashing the garlic along with the potatoes.

3 pounds Yukon Gold potatoes,
  peeled and cut into 1-inch chunks
1 cup skim milk, or more if needed

Salt to taste
Freshly ground black pepper to taste

Place the potatoes in a large saucepan and add water to cover. Bring to a boil and simmer for about 15 minutes or until the potatoes are tender and can easily be pierced with a fork. Drain the potatoes and return to the pan. With a potato masher, mash the potatoes with the milk, adding more if necessary to get a smooth consistency. Season with salt and pepper.

**Makes 8 servings, save half for Monday**
**Per serving: 144 calories, 4g protein, 32g carbohydrate, 0 fat,**
**0 cholesterol, 23mg sodium**
**Exchanges: 2 starch**

# Broccoli

2 1/4 pounds fresh broccoli

Prepare the broccoli by washing and then cutting into small florets. The stems can be peeled and sliced. Place the florets and stems in a microwave-safe bowl, cover, and microwave on high for 4 to 5 minutes. The broccoli should be tender but not mushy.

**Makes 8 servings, save half for Monday**
**Per serving: 30 calories, 3g protein, 5g carbohydrate, 0 fat,**
**0 cholesterol, 28mg sodium**
**Exchanges: 1 vegetable**

# Rotelle

12 ounces rotelle pasta

Boil pasta in water according to package directions. Save for Tuesday.

# Cream of Broccoli Soup

The mashed potatoes in this recipe give the soup a thick,
creamy texture without adding cream.

1/2 recipe mashed potatoes, saved
from Sunday

1/2 recipe cooked broccoli, saved
from Sunday

15-ounce can reduced-sodium
chicken broth

8 ounces fat-free sour cream

8-ounce package Sargento Light
reduced-fat shredded cheddar
cheese

Freshly ground black pepper to taste

In a large saucepan, combine the potatoes, broccoli, and broth. Bring to a
boil and simmer for about 5 minutes. With a potato masher, mash the
broccoli until broken up into small pieces (you can also use a hand-held
blender for a smoother texture). Add the sour cream and cheese. Continue to heat and stir until cheese is melted. Season with black pepper.

**Makes 4 servings**
Per serving: 393 calories, 28g protein, 50g carbohydrate, 11g fat,
21mg cholesterol, 521mg sodium
Exchanges: 2 1/2 meat, 2 1/2 starch, 1 vegetable, 1 fat

# Italian Bread

1/2 pound Italian bread

**Makes 4 servings**
Per serving: 154 calories, 5g protein, 28g carbohydrate, 2g fat,
0 cholesterol, 331mg sodium
Exchanges: 2 starch

# Green Salad

10-ounce bag ready-to-eat salad

1/2 cup bottled fat-free salad dressing

In a large serving bowl combine the salad and dressing.

**Makes 4 servings**
Per serving: 21 calories, 1g protein, 4g carbohydrate, 0 fat,
0 cholesterol, 296mg sodium
Exchanges: 1 vegetable

# Rotelle with Meat Sauce

1/2 recipe meatloaf, saved from
  Sunday
26-ounce jar Healthy Choice
  pasta sauce

Cooked rotelle, saved from Sunday
Grated Parmesan cheese, optional

In a large saucepan over medium-high heat, combine the meatloaf and
sauce, breaking up the meatloaf with a spoon. Add the rotelle pasta and
continue to cook until heated through. Serve with grated Parmesan
cheese if desired.

**Makes 4 servings**
**Per serving: 534 calories, 39g protein, 79g carbohydrate, 7g fat,**
**69mg cholesterol, 900mg sodium**
**Exchanges: 3 meat, 3 1/2 starch, 2 vegetable, 1 fat**

# Green Beans

16-ounce package frozen Italian-style green beans

Cook the green beans in the microwave according to package directions.

**Makes 4 servings**
**Per serving: 27 calories, 1g protein, 6g carbohydrate, 0 fat,**
**0 cholesterol, 13mg sodium**
**Exchanges: 1 vegetable**

# Bean Burritos

8-count package fat-free tortillas
16-ounce can fat-free refried beans
2 medium tomatoes, chopped

4 ounces Sargento Light reduced-fat
 shredded mozzarella cheese
8-ounce jar picante sauce

Spread the refried beans, tomatoes, and cheese on each tortilla. Roll the tortillas into a burrito shape and heat in the microwave for a few minutes until heated through and the cheese melts. Top with picante sauce.

**Makes 4 servings**
**Per serving: 292 calories, 17g protein, 47g carbohydrate, 4g fat,**
**10mg cholesterol, 1293mg sodium**
**Exchanges: 1 meat, 2 starch, 1/2 vegetable**

# Corn Salsa

16-ounce package frozen kernel
 corn

16-ounce jar salsa

Defrost the corn in the microwave. In a serving bowl mix together the corn and salsa.

**Makes 4 servings**
**Per serving: 155 calories, 7g protein, 35g carbohydrate, 0 fat,**
**0 cholesterol, 877mg sodium**
**Exchanges: 1 1/2 starch, 2 vegetable**

## Thursday

# Italian Bread Salad with Smoked Turkey

8 ounces Italian bread, cut into bite-sized pieces

10-ounce package ready-to-eat Italian blend salad

2 ripe tomatoes, sliced

1 medium cucumber, sliced

1 red onion, peeled and sliced

1/2 cup pitted kalamata or Greek-style olives

8 ounces smoked turkey breast, cut into bite-sized pieces

1/2 cup fat-free Italian salad dressing

In a large serving bowl, toss together all the ingredients.

**Makes 4 servings**
**Per serving: 313 calories, 18g protein, 44g carbohydrate, 7g fat,**
**20mg cholesterol, 1385mg sodium**
**Exchanges: 2 meat, 2 starch, 2 vegetable, 1 fat**

## Friday

# Tuna Melt Sandwich

2 7-ounce cans tuna packed in olive oil, drained

2 tablespoons fat-free mayonnaise

1 tablespoon capers

2 tablespoons lemon juice

Freshly ground black pepper to taste

4 ounces Sargento Light reduced-fat shredded mozzarella cheese

4 sandwich rolls

Combine the tuna, mayonnaise, capers, lemon juice, and pepper. Spread the tuna mixture onto the 4 sandwich rolls and top with cheese. Heat in the microwave for 1 to 2 minutes until heated through and cheese melts.

**Makes 4 servings**
**Per serving: 341 calories, 32g protein, 24g carbohydrate, 11g fat,**
**23mg cholesterol, 766mg sodium**
**Exchanges: 4 meat, 2 starch**

# Pepper Salad

16-ounce package frozen mixed          1/4 cup fat-free Italian salad dressing
  pepper strips

Defrost the peppers in the microwave. Drain excess water from peppers.
In a serving bowl combine the peppers and salad dressing.

Makes 4 servings
Per serving: 27 calories, 1g protein, 5g carbohydrate, 0 fat,
0 cholesterol, 201mg sodium
Exchanges: 1 vegetable

# Week 5

### Sunday
Roast Chicken with Gravy
Baked Potatoes
Cranberry Sauce
Butternut Squash

### Monday
Hot Chicken Sandwiches
Mixed Vegetables

### Tuesday
Potato and Asparagus Frittata
French Bread

### Wednesday
Harvest Soup
Cheese Toast

### Thursday
Oriental Chicken Noodle Salad

### Friday
Shrimp Scampi Pizza
Spinach Salad

# Week 5

## Staples

Extra virgin olive oil
Sesame oil
Rice vinegar
Soy sauce
Sugar
Grated Parmesan cheese
Bottled fat-free poppy seed salad
   dressing

### Seasonings
Garlic powder
Ground ginger
Ground cinnamon
Ground nutmeg
Black pepper
Dried rosemary

# Week 5

**Fresh Produce**

6 medium russet potatoes

3 ripe tomatoes

1 cucumber

1 red onion

6-ounce package ready-to-eat baby spinach

6 pounds butternut squash

2 apples

**Canned and Bottled Foods**

Small jar peeled and minced garlic

11-ounce can mandarin oranges

Small jar applesauce

8-ounce can cranberry sauce

12-ounce jar fat-free gravy

15-ounce can reduced-sodium chicken broth

Small jar pizza sauce

Small bottle hoisin sauce

8-ounce can sliced water chestnuts

**Breads and Grains**

10-ounce prepared Italian pizza shell

12-ounce package linguine

1/2-pound loaf good quality French bread

8 slices sandwich bread

**Frozen Foods**

16-ounce package asparagus spears

6-ounce package snow peas

16-ounce package mixed vegetables

Small package diced onion

**Dairy Foods**

16-ounce carton egg substitute

8-ounce package Sargento Light reduced-fat Italian blend shredded cheese

4 slices reduced-fat American cheese

Skim milk

8-ounce container fat-free sour cream

**Meats, Poultry, and Seafood**

7-pound oven stuffer roasting chicken

1/4 pound cooked and peeled shrimp

# Week 5

## Sunday

The potatoes and chicken can cook in the oven at the same time. Place the potatoes in the oven about 1 1/2 hours before the chicken is done.

## Roast Chicken

The chicken can be stuffed as an option. This would be a good opportunity to use any leftover corn bread you may have in the freezer from Week Two. Take all the chicken off the bones before saving in the refrigerator to help make weeknight meals easier.

**7-pound oven stuffer roasting chicken**

Preheat oven to 350°. Remove giblets and rinse chicken inside and out. Stuff if desired. Place in a large roasting pan breast side up. Roast in the oven for 2 1/2 to 2 3/4 hours or until internal temperature reaches 165° using an instant-read thermometer. Add 20 to 25 minutes cooking time if chicken is stuffed. Let stand 15 minutes before carving. Save pan drippings to make gravy.

**Makes 12 servings, save one-third for Monday and one-third for Thursday**
**Per serving (without skin): 208 calories, 39g protein, 0 carbohydrate, 5g fat,**
**107mg cholesterol, 92mg sodium**
**Exchanges: 3 meat**

## Baked Potatoes

**6 medium baking potatoes, such as russet potatoes**

Scrub potatoes well using a vegetable scrub brush. Pierce each potato several times with a fork. Bake at 350° for about 1 1/2 hours or until the potatoes can be easily pierced with a fork.

**Makes 6 servings, save 2 potatoes for Tuesday**
**Per serving: 220 calories, 5g protein, 51g carbohydrate, 0 fat,**
**0 cholesterol, 16mg sodium**
**Exchanges: 2 1/2 starch**

# Gravy

I was never good at making gravy from scratch so I cheat, and nobody knows the difference.

**Pan drippings from roast chicken     12-ounce jar fat-free gravy**

Pour pan drippings into a measuring cup with a bottom pour spout. When all the fat comes up to the top of the measuring cup, pour the broth from the bottom back into the pan and discard the fat. Add the jar of gravy and stir over medium-high heat, breaking up any brown bits from the bottom of the pan. Cook until heated through.

**Makes 8 servings, save half for Monday**
**Per serving: 10 calories, 1g protein, 3g carbohydrate, 0 fat, 0 cholesterol, 350mg sodium**
**Exchanges: free food**

# Cranberry Sauce

**8-ounce can cranberry sauce**

Chill the cranberry sauce in the refrigerator.

**Makes 4 servings**
**Per serving: 78 calories, 0 protein, 20g carbohydrate, 0 fat,**
**0 cholesterol, 15mg sodium**
**Exchanges: 1 fruit**

# Butternut Squash

**6 pounds fresh butternut squash     Ground nutmeg to taste**
**Ground cinnamon to taste**

Peel squash and cut into chunks. Place in a large saucepan and barely cover with water. Bring to a boil, reduce heat, and simmer for about 5 to 10 minutes or until squash can easily be pierced with a fork. Drain squash and mash with a dash of cinnamon and nutmeg.

**Makes 8 servings, save half for Wednesday**
**Per serving: 62 calories, 1g protein, 16g carbohydrate, 0 fat,**
**0 cholesterol, 6mg sodium**
**Exchanges: 1 starch**

# Noodles

**12 ounces linguine**

Boil pasta according to package directions. Save for Thursday.

# Hot Chicken Sandwiches

8 slices sandwich bread

1/3 recipe roast chicken, saved from
  Sunday

1/2 recipe gravy, saved from Sunday

Place chicken and gravy on 8 slices of bread. Place sandwiches on a microwave-safe plate and cover with plastic wrap. Microwave on high for 2 to 3 minutes or until heated through.

**Makes 4 servings**
**Per serving: 248 calories, 24g protein, 29g carbohydrate, 4g fat,**
**52mg cholesterol, 699mg sodium**
**Exchanges: 3 meat, 2 starch**

# Mixed Vegetables

16-ounce package frozen mixed vegetables

Cook vegetables in the microwave according to package directions.

**Makes 4 servings**
**Per serving: 67 calories, 3g protein, 15g carbohydrate, 0 fat,**
**0 cholesterol, 40mg sodium**
**Exchanges: 3 vegetable**

# Potato and Asparagus Frittata

1 teaspoon olive oil

2 cooked potatoes, saved from
  Sunday, cut into 1/2-inch pieces

16-ounce package frozen asparagus
  spears

16-ounce carton egg substitute

1/4 teaspoon garlic powder

1/2 teaspoon dried rosemary

Freshly ground black pepper to taste

1/4 cup grated Parmesan cheese

2 ripe tomatoes, chopped

1/4 pound good quality French bread

Preheat the broiler. In a large nonstick, ovenproof skillet, heat the potatoes in the oil over medium-high heat for 1 to 2 minutes or until they start to brown. Defrost the asparagus in the microwave and add to the skillet. Reduce to low heat, and add the egg substitute to the pan. Sprinkle the seasonings and Parmesan cheese over the eggs. Cover the pan and cook for about 5 minutes or until the underside is golden brown. Place the skillet under the broiler for 1 to 2 minutes or until the top of the frittata is puffy and golden brown. Serve with chopped tomatoes and a slice of French bread.

**Makes 4 servings**
**Per serving: 310 calories, 22g protein, 48g carbohydrate, 4g fat,**
**4mg cholesterol, 462mg sodium**
**Exchanges: 2 meat, 2 1/2 starch, 1 1/2 vegetable**

Make the cheese toast while the soup is simmering.

# Harvest Soup

1/2 recipe butternut squash, saved from Sunday

2 apples, cored and minced fine

15-ounce can reduced-sodium chicken broth

1 cup skim milk

1/2 cup applesauce

1/2 cup frozen diced onion

1/2 teaspoon ground ginger

Freshly ground black pepper to taste

Ground nutmeg to taste

1/2 cup fat-free sour cream

Combine all ingredients except sour cream in a medium saucepan. Bring to a boil, reduce heat, and simmer for a few minutes or until apples are tender. Top each bowl of soup with 2 tablespoons sour cream.

Makes 4 servings
Per serving: 192 calories, 7g protein, 41g carbohydrate, 2g fat,
1mg cholesterol, 83mg sodium
Exchanges: 2 starch

# Cheese Toast

4 slices good quality French bread     4 slices reduced-fat American cheese

Preheat the broiler. Place a slice of cheese on each slice of bread. Place under the broiler for 1 to 2 minutes or until cheese is melted and golden brown.

Makes 4 servings
Per serving: 150 calories, 11g protein, 13g carbohydrate, 5g fat,
20mg cholesterol, 375mg sodium
Exchanges: 1 meat, 1 starch

# Oriental Chicken Noodle Salad

You can also use bottled reduced-fat Oriental dressing instead of making your own.

1/4 cup rice vinegar

2 teaspoons sesame oil

2 tablespoons soy sauce

1 tablespoon hoisin sauce

1 tablespoon sugar

1/8 teaspoon garlic powder

1/8 teaspoon ground ginger

Dash cayenne pepper or to taste

6-ounce package frozen snow peas

Cooked noodles, saved from Sunday

1/3 recipe roast chicken, saved from Sunday, cut in bite-size pieces

1 cucumber, peeled and chopped

1 tomato, chopped

8-ounce can sliced water chestnuts, drained

In a large serving bowl, whisk together the vinegar, oil, soy sauce, hoisin sauce, sugar, and seasonings. Defrost the snow peas in the microwave. Add the peas and remaining ingredients to the dressing in the serving bowl and toss well to combine.

**Makes 4 servings**
**Per serving: 528 calories, 39g protein, 74g carbohydrate, 7g fat, 72mg cholesterol, 591mg sodium**
**Exchanges: 3 meat, 3 starch, 2 vegetable**

## Friday

Toss the salad together while the pizza broils.

# Shrimp Scampi Pizza

10-ounce prepared Italian
   pizza shell
1 cup prepared pizza sauce
3 teaspoons or more peeled and
   minced garlic (bottled is fine)

1/4 pound cooked and peeled shrimp
8 ounces Sargento Light reduced-fat
   Italian blend shredded cheese

Preheat the broiler. Place pizza shell on a pizza pan or baking sheet.
Spread the pizza sauce and garlic over the shell. Distribute the shrimp
over the pizza sauce. If desired you can slice the shrimp in half lengthwise
to cover more area. Sprinkle the cheese over the top. Place under the
broiler for a few minutes until the cheese is melted and browned.

**Makes 4 servings**
**Per serving: 496 calories, 37g protein, 54g carbohydrate, 10g fat,**
**86mg cholesterol, 998mg sodium**
**Exchanges: 3 1/2 meat, 3 starch, 1/2 vegetable, 1 1/2 fat**

# Spinach Salad

6-ounce package ready-to-eat baby
   spinach
11-ounce can mandarin oranges,
   drained

1 red onion, peeled and sliced
1/2 cup bottled fat-free poppy seed
   salad dressing

In a large serving bowl toss all ingredients together until combined.

**Makes 4 servings**
**Per serving: 93 calories, 2g protein, 21g carbohydrate, 0 fat,**
**0 cholesterol, 184mg sodium**
**Exchanges: 2 vegetable, 1/2 fruit**

# Week 6

## Menu

### Sunday
Roast Beef with Gravy
Mashed Potatoes
Carrots
Broccoli

### Monday
Shepherd's Pie

### Tuesday
Couscous Primavera

### Wednesday
Oriental Beef and Broccoli with
    Noodles

### Thursday
Greek Pizza
Green Salad

### Friday
Smoked Turkey Bagel Sandwich
Cold Beet Borscht

# Week 6

## Staples

Peanut oil or canola oil
Lemon juice
Dijon or grainy-type mustard
Bottled favorite fat-free salad dressing

**Seasonings**
Crushed oregano
Paprika
Salt
Black pepper

# Week 6

## Shopping List

**Fresh Produce**

3 pounds Yukon Gold potatoes

2 pounds carrots

2 1/4 pounds broccoli

4 ripe tomatoes

1 large white onion

1 red onion

10-ounce bag ready-to-eat salad

**Canned and Bottled Foods**

12-ounce jar fat-free gravy

33-ounce jar beet borscht

7-ounce can sliced mushrooms

15-ounce can kidney beans

Small jar pitted kalamata or
    Greek-style olives

Bottle stir-fry sauce

**Breads and Grains**

5.9-ounce box Near East Parmesan-
    flavored couscous

12-ounce package angel hair pasta

10-ounce prepared Italian pizza shell

4 medium bagels

**Frozen Foods**

2 10-ounce packages peas

16-ounce package mixed pepper strips

**Dairy Foods**

8 ounces crumbled feta cheese

Small container fat-free sour cream

**Meats, Poultry, and Seafood**

2 1/2 pound lean oven roast, such as
    eye of round

8 ounces sliced smoked turkey breast

# Week 6

The potatoes and vegetables can be prepared while the roast beef cooks. To make weeknight cooking easier, cut the leftover roast beef into bite-sized pieces before storing in the refrigerator.

## Roast Beef

2 pounds lean oven roast, such as        1 large onion, peeled and chopped
   eye of round

Preheat the oven to 300°. Rinse the beef and place in a roasting pan with the onion. Roast in the oven for about 1 1/2 hours or until the internal temperature reaches 160° using an instant-read thermometer. Let stand for 15 minutes before carving into slices.

Makes 12 servings, save one-third for Monday and one-third for Wednesday
Per serving: 160 calories, 21g protein, 0 carbohydrate, 8g fat,
50mg cholesterol, 37mg sodium
Exchanges: 3 meat

## Gravy

Again, here is my cheating method of making gravy.

Pan drippings from roast beef        12-ounce jar fat-free gravy

Pour the pan drippings into a measuring cup with a bottom pour spout. Try to leave the browned bits of onion in the pan. When all the fat comes up to the top of the measuring cup, pour the broth from the bottom back into the pan and discard the fat. Add the jar of gravy and stir over medium-high heat, breaking up any brown bits from the bottom of the pan. Continue cooking until heated through.

Makes 8 servings, save half for Monday
Per serving: 10 calories, 1g protein, 3g carbohydrate, 0 fat,
0 cholesterol, 350mg sodium
Exchanges: free food

# Mashed Potatoes

3 pounds Yukon Gold potatoes, peeled and cut into 1-inch chunks

1 cup skim milk, or more if needed

Salt to taste

Freshly ground black pepper to taste

Place the potatoes in a large saucepan and add water to cover. Bring to a boil and simmer for about 15 minutes or until the potatoes are tender and can easily be pierced with a fork. Drain the potatoes and return to the pan. With a potato masher, mash the potatoes with the milk, adding more if necessary to get a smooth consistency. Season with salt and pepper.

Makes 8 servings, save half for Monday
Per serving: 144 calories, 4g protein, 32g carbohydrate, 0 fat,
0 cholesterol, 23mg sodium
Exchanges: 2 starch

# Carrots

2 pounds carrots, peeled and sliced into 1/4-inch rounds

Place carrots and 1 tablespoon water in a microwave-safe bowl and cover. Microwave on high for about 5 minutes until tender but not mushy.

Makes 12 servings, save one-third for Monday and one-third for Tuesday
Per serving: 33 calories, 1g protein, 8g carbohydrate, 0 fat,
0 cholesterol, 49mg sodium
Exchanges: 1 vegetable

# Broccoli

2 1/4 pounds fresh broccoli

Wash the broccoli and cut into small florets. The stems can be peeled and sliced. Place the florets and stems in a microwave-safe bowl and cover. Microwave on high for 4 to 5 minutes until the broccoli is tender but not mushy.

Makes 8 servings, save half for Wednesday
Per serving: 30 calories, 3g protein, 5g carbohydrate, 0 fat,
0 cholesterol, 28mg sodium
Exchanges: 1 vegetable

# Shepherd's Pie

My mother and grandmother always used leftover roast beef by making shepherd's pie. It is a simple but delicious recipe. Sometimes to save time I'll assemble the pie on Sunday before putting the leftovers away.

1/3 recipe roast beef, cut into bite-sized pieces, saved from Sunday

1/2 recipe carrots, saved from Sunday

1/2 recipe gravy, saved from Sunday

10-ounce package frozen peas

1/2 recipe mashed potatoes, saved from Sunday

1/2 teaspoon paprika

In a casserole pan or deep dish pie plate, combine the roast beef, carrots, gravy, and peas. Spread the mashed potatoes on top of the mixture. Sprinkle the paprika over the potatoes. Cover and microwave on high for about 8 minutes or until heated through. You can also heat the pie, uncovered, in a 400° oven for 30 minutes, but I never have time to wait that long.

Makes 4 servings
Per serving: 410 calories, 30g protein, 55g carbohydrate, 8g fat,
50mg cholesterol, 529mg sodium
Exchanges: 3 meat, 3 starch, 1 1/2 vegetable

# Couscous Primavera

5.9-ounce box Near East Parmesan-
   flavored couscous
10-ounce package frozen peas
1/3 recipe carrots, saved from
   Sunday

1 ripe tomato, chopped
15-ounce can kidney beans, drained
1 teaspoon lemon juice

In a large saucepan bring 1 1/4 cups water to a boil. Add couscous with spice packet, peas, carrots, tomato, and beans. Cover, remove from heat, and let stand for 5 minutes. Add lemon juice and fluff mixture with a fork.

**Makes 4 servings**
**Per serving: 311 calories, 15g protein, 63g carbohydrate, 1g fat,**
**0 cholesterol, 875mg sodium**
**Exchanges: 1 meat, 3 starch, 2 vegetable**

# Oriental Beef and Broccoli with Noodles

12 ounces angel hair pasta

1 teaspoon peanut oil or canola oil

1/2 recipe broccoli, saved from Sunday

7-ounce can sliced mushrooms, drained

1/3 recipe roast beef, cut into bite-sized pieces, saved from Sunday

16-ounce package frozen mixed pepper strips

1 cup stir-fry sauce

Cook pasta in 2 quarts of boiling water for 2 to 3 minutes; drain and place in a large serving bowl. While the pasta is cooking, stir-fry the broccoli, mushrooms, beef, and peppers in the oil for a few minutes until heated through. Add the stir-fry sauce. Serve over the noodles.

Makes 4 servings
Per serving: 599 calories, 42g protein, 84g carbohydrate, 10g fat,
73mg cholesterol, 707mg sodium
Exchanges: 3 meat, 3 starch, 2 vegetable

# Greek Pizza

10-ounce prepared Italian pizza
  shell

2 ripe tomatoes, sliced thin

1 teaspoon crushed oregano

8 ounces crumbled feta cheese

1/2 cup pitted kalamata or Greek-
  style olives

Preheat the broiler. Place the pizza shell on a pizza pan or baking pan. Spread the tomatoes, oregano, cheese, and olives on the pizza shell. Place under the broiler for a few minutes or until the top is browned and the cheese is melting.

**Makes 4 servings**
**Per serving: 477 calories, 23g protein, 55g carbohydrate, 16g fat,**
**74mg cholesterol, 1311mg sodium**
**Exchanges: 1 1/2 meat, 3 starch, 1/2 vegetable, 2 fat**

# Green Salad

10-ounce package ready-to-eat
  salad

1/2 cup of favorite fat-free salad
  dressing

Toss together in a large salad bowl.

**Makes 4 servings**
**Per serving: 21 calories, 1g protein, 4g carbohydrates, 0 fat,**
**0 cholesterol, 296mg sodium**
**Exchanges: 1 vegetable**

# Smoked Turkey Bagel Sandwich

4 medium-size bagels

8 ounces sliced smoked turkey
  breast

1 ripe tomato, sliced

1 red onion, peeled and sliced

Dijon or grainy-type mustard

Divide the ingredients among the bagels to make sandwiches.

**Makes 4 servings**
**Per serving: 318 calories, 19g protein, 55g carbohydrate, 2g fat,**
**23mg cholesterol, 1226mg sodium**
**Exchanges: 2 meat, 3 starch, 1/2 vegetable**

# Cold Beet Borscht

33-ounce jar beet borscht, chilled
  in the refrigerator

Small container fat-free sour cream

Divide the borscht into 4 bowls and top each serving with 2 tablespoons of sour cream.

**Makes 4 servings**
**Per serving: 95 calories, 4g protein, 20 carbohydrate, 0 fat,**
**0 cholesterol, 485mg sodium**
**Exchanges: 3 vegetable**

# Week 7

### Sunday
Barbecued Chicken Breast
Spinach
Barley Pilaf

### Monday
Barbecued Chicken Pizza
Green Salad

### Tuesday
Black Bean Soup
Salad Stuffed Pita

### Wednesday
Barbecued Chicken Sandwich
Coleslaw

### Thursday
Italian Sub Sandwich
Corn Relish

### Friday
Capellini Carbonara with Ham and
    Peas

# Week 7

## Staples

Bottled fat-free Italian salad dressing
Bottled favorite fat-free salad dressing
Extra virgin olive oil
Dijon or grainy-type mustard
Red wine vinegar

**Seasonings**
Black pepper
Garlic powder
Ground cumin

# Week 7

**Fresh Produce**

2 pounds spinach

2 10-ounce packages ready-to-eat salad

2 ripe tomatoes

10-ounce package coleslaw mix (shredded cabbage)

2 green bell peppers

3 onions

2 carrots

**Canned and Bottled Foods**

Bottled barbecue sauce

Bottled fat-free coleslaw dressing

7-ounce jar roasted sweet red peppers

Small jar green olive salad

15-ounce can diced tomatoes

15-ounce can reduced-sodium beef broth

15-ounce can reduced-sodium vegetable or chicken broth

8-ounce can evaporated skim milk

**Breads and Grains**

10-ounce prepared Italian pizza shell

4-count package torpedo rolls

4-count package sandwich rolls

2 large pita bread rounds

12-ounce package angel hair pasta

Package Quick Quaker barley

**Frozen Foods**

16-ounce package kernel corn

16-ounce package peas

Small package diced onion

Small package diced green peppers

2 14-ounce packages black beans

**Dairy Foods**

8-ounce package Sargento Light reduced-fat shredded mozzarella cheese

4 ounces sliced low-fat cheese

4-ounce container egg substitute

Grated Parmesan cheese

Small container fat-free sour cream

**Meats, Poultry, and Seafood**

8 ounces lean ham

2 1/2 pounds boneless and skinless chicken breasts (10 halves)

4 ounces each Thin 'n Trim roast beef and salami

# Week 7

## Sunday

The barley and spinach can be prepared while the chicken cooks.

## Barbecued Chicken Breasts

You could also barbecue the chicken breasts on an outdoor grill.

2 1/2 pounds boneless and skinless chicken breasts (10 halves)

1 cup barbecue sauce

1 onion, peeled and sliced thin

1 green bell pepper, cored and sliced thin

Preheat the oven to 350°. Rinse chicken and pat dry with paper towels. Place chicken in a large baking pan lined with foil. Pour sauce and vegetables over chicken. Place another sheet of foil over the chicken and bake for about 45 minutes or until the internal temperature of the chicken reaches 165° using an instant-read thermometer.

Makes 10 servings, save two breasts for Monday and four for Wednesday
Per serving: 166 calories, 25g protein, 8g carbohydrate, 3g fat,
69mg cholesterol, 428mg sodium
Exchanges: 3 meat

## Spinach

2 pounds fresh spinach

Red wine vinegar, optional

Wash spinach and trim stems. Place in a microwave-safe bowl and cover. Microwave on high for about 3 to 5 minutes. The spinach should be wilted but not mushy. Sprinkle with red wine vinegar, if desired.

Makes 4 servings
Per serving: 40 calories, 5g protein, 6g carbohydrate, 0 fat,
0 cholesterol, 122mg sodium
Exchanges: 1 vegetable

# Barley Pilaf

This is a nice change from rice or potatoes. It is also good served cold with some leftover cooked vegetables and fat-free Italian salad dressing.

1 teaspoon olive oil

1 onion, peeled and chopped

1 green pepper, cored and chopped

2 carrots, peeled and chopped

15-ounce can reduced-sodium vegetable or chicken broth

1/4 cup water

1 cup Quick Quaker barley

Freshly ground black pepper to taste

In a large saucepan sauté the onion, pepper, and carrots in the olive oil until slightly browned. Add the broth and water and bring to a boil. Add the barley, cover, and simmer for about 12 minutes. Let stand for 5 minutes. Season with black pepper.

**Makes 4 servings**
**Per serving: 177 calories, 6g protein, 33g carbohydrate, 3g fat,**
**0 cholesterol, 24mg sodium**
**Exchanges: 2 starch**

# Barbecued Chicken Pizza

10-ounce prepared Italian
pizza shell

1/3 cup barbecue sauce

2 barbecued chicken breasts with
onions and peppers, saved from
Sunday, chopped

8-ounce package Sargento Light
reduced-fat shredded mozzarella
cheese

Preheat the broiler. Place the pizza shell on a pizza pan or cookie sheet. Spread the barbecue sauce on the pizza shell. Spread the chicken and cheese over the sauce. Place under the broiler for a few minutes until cheese melts and browns.

**Makes 4 servings**
**Per serving: 421 calories, 36g protein, 40g carbohydrate, 11g fat,**
**59mg cholesterol, 1122mg sodium**
**Exchanges: 3 1/2 meat, 2 1/2 starch, 1 fat**

# Green Salad

10-ounce bag ready-to-eat salad          1/2 cup fat-free salad dressing

In a large serving bowl combine the salad and dressing.

**Makes 4 servings**
**Per serving: 21 calories, 1g protein, 4g carbohydrate, 0 fat,**
**0 cholesterol, 296mg sodium**
**Exchanges: 1 vegetable**

# Black Bean Soup

1/2 cup frozen diced onion

1/2 cup frozen diced green pepper

2 14-ounce packages frozen black beans

15-ounce can reduced-sodium beef broth

15-ounce can diced tomatoes

1 teaspoon ground cumin

1/2 teaspoon garlic powder

Fat-free sour cream, optional

In a large saucepan combine all ingredients except sour cream. Heat over high heat for several minutes until heated through. Top each serving with 2 tablespoons sour cream, if desired.

**Makes 4 servings**
**Per serving: 278 calories, 18g protein, 48g carbohydrate, 2g fat,**
**0 cholesterol, 223mg sodium**
**Exchanges: 1 meat, 2 1/2 starch, 1 1/2 vegetable**

# Salad Stuffed Pita

10-ounce package ready-to-eat salad

1/2 cup fat-free salad dressing

2 large pita bread rounds

Combine the salad and dressing. Slice the pita bread in half. Stuff each half with the salad.

**Makes 4 servings**
**Per serving: 131 calories, 3g protein, 28g carbohydrate, 0 fat,**
**0 cholesterol, 536mg sodium**
**Exchanges: 1 starch, 1 vegetable**

# Barbecued Chicken Sandwich

4 barbecued chicken breast halves,
  saved from Sunday
4 sandwich rolls

2 ripe tomatoes, sliced
Barbecue sauce, optional

Heat the chicken in the microwave for a few minutes until heated through. Place each chicken breast half in a sandwich roll along with sliced tomatoes. Top with additional barbecue sauce if desired.

**Makes 4 servings**
Per serving: 302 calories, 29g protein, 32g carbohydrate, 5g fat,
69mg cholesterol, 675mg sodium
Exchanges: 3 meat, 2 starch

# Coleslaw

10-ounce package coleslaw mix
  (shredded cabbage)

1/2 cup fat-free coleslaw dressing

In a large serving bowl, combine the cabbage and dressing until mixed well.

**Makes 4 servings**
Per serving: 40 calories, 1g protein, 8g carbohydrate, 0 fat,
0 cholesterol, 224mg sodium
Exchanges: 1 1/2 vegetable

# Italian Sub Sandwich

4 torpedo rolls

4 ounces each Thin 'n Trim roast
  beef and salami

4 ounces sliced low-fat cheese

1/2 cup green olive salad

1/2 cup fat-free Italian salad dressing

Slice each roll horizontally and fill with the remaining ingredients.

**Makes 4 servings**
**Per serving: 401 calories, 24g protein, 59g carbohydrate, 9g fat,**
**30mg cholesterol, 2060mg sodium**
**Exchanges: 3 meat, 3 starch, 1 1/2 fat**

# Corn Relish

16-ounce package frozen corn

7-ounce jar roasted sweet red peppers,
  drained and chopped

1/2 cup fat-free Italian salad dressing

Defrost the corn in the microwave. Combine all ingredients together in a
large serving bowl.

**Makes 4 servings**
**Per serving: 134 calories, 4g protein, 32g carbohydrate, 1g fat,**
**0 cholesterol, 369mg sodium**
**Exchanges: 1 1/2 starch, 1 vegetable**

# Capellini Carbonara with Ham and Peas

12-ounce package angel hair pasta

16-ounce package frozen peas

8 ounces lean ham, cut into bite-
  sized pieces

1/4 cup egg substitute

1/2 cup evaporated skim milk,
  or more if needed

1/2 cup grated Parmesan cheese

1/2 teaspoon garlic powder

Freshly ground black pepper to taste

In a large saucepan cook the pasta in 2 quarts of boiling water for 2 to 3 minutes. Place the peas in a colander and drain the pasta in the colander directly over the peas to defrost them. Return the pasta and peas to the saucepan. Add the remaining ingredients to the pan and cook over low heat for a minute. Add more milk if necessary.

**Makes 4 servings**
**Per serving: 557 calories, 35g protein, 87g carbohydrate, 7g fat,**
**35mg cholesterol, 854mg sodium**
**Exchanges: 3 meat, 3 1/2 starch, 2 vegetable**

# Week 8

### Sunday
Spaghetti and Meatballs
Green Beans

### Monday
Meatball Sub Sandwich
Green Bean Vinaigrette

### Tuesday
Minestrone Soup

### Wednesday
Meatball Pizza
Green Salad

### Thursday
Hot Dog on Roll
Baked Beans
Sauerkraut

### Friday
Pan Bagna

# Week 8

## Staples

Bread crumbs
Grated Parmesan cheese
Bottled fat-free Italian salad dressing
Bottled favorite fat-free salad dressing
Red wine vinegar
Mustard

**Seasonings**
Garlic powder
Dried basil
Crushed oregano
Crushed thyme
Black pepper

# Week 8

## Fresh Produce

4 cloves garlic (or use bottled)

1 onion

1 red onion

1 carrot

2 pounds green beans

10-ounce package ready-to-eat salad

1 ripe tomato

## Canned and Bottled Foods

16-ounce can fat-free vegetarian-style baked beans

14.4-ounce can sauerkraut

2 28-ounce cans crushed tomatoes

28-ounce can diced tomatoes

6-ounce can tomato paste

Small jar pizza sauce

7-ounce jar roasted sweet red peppers

15-ounce can kidney beans

7-ounce can tuna packed in olive oil

15-ounce can reduced-sodium beef broth

## Breads and Grains

4 hot dog rolls

4 torpedo rolls

8-inch round loaf good quality Italian bread

10-ounce prepared Italian pizza shell

Package of soup-mac pasta

12-ounce package spaghetti

## Frozen Foods

10-ounce package chopped kale or spinach

16-ounce package Italian-style mixed vegetables

14-ounce package white beans

## Dairy Foods

4-ounce carton egg substitute

8 ounces Sargento Light reduced-fat shredded mozzarella cheese

## Meats, Poultry, and Seafood

14-ounce package Healthy Choice low-fat beef franks

3 pounds ground turkey breast or 95% lean ground beef

# Week 8

This is my family's favorite week. Simmer the sauce and boil the spaghetti while the meatballs cook in the oven.

## Meatballs

3 pounds ground turkey breast or
  95% lean ground beef

1/2 cup egg substitute

1/2 cup water

1 teaspoon dried basil

1/4 teaspoon ground black pepper

1 cup bread crumbs

Preheat the oven to 375°. In a large bowl, combine the ground turkey or beef, egg, water, basil, black pepper, and bread crumbs. Shape the mixture into 72 1-inch meatballs. Place meatballs on foil-lined baking sheets and bake for about 20 minutes. Save 8 meatballs for Wednesday before adding to the sauce.

## Marinara Sauce

When I have leftover wine around, I'll add about 1/2 cup to the vegetables and reduce it by half before adding the tomatoes.

1 teaspoon olive oil

2 to 4 cloves garlic, peeled and
  minced (bottled is fine)

1 onion, peeled and minced

1 carrot, peeled and minced

2 28-ounce cans crushed tomatoes

6-ounce can tomato paste

1 tablespoon crushed oregano

1 teaspoon dried basil

Freshly ground black pepper to taste

In a large nonstick skillet sauté the garlic, onion, and carrot in the olive oil over medium-high heat until the vegetables are slightly brown and wilted. Add the crushed tomatoes, tomato paste, oregano, basil, and black pepper. Bring to a boil, reduce heat, and simmer for 15 minutes. Add the cooked meatballs to the sauce. Save half of meatballs and sauce for Monday before combining with the spaghetti.

# Spaghetti

12-ounce package spaghetti          Grated Parmesan cheese, optional

Serve the remaining meatballs and sauce over 12 ounces of spaghetti cooked according to package directions. Serve with grated Parmesan cheese if desired.

**Makes 4 servings**
**Per serving: 650 calories, 52g protein, 92g carbohydrate, 6g fat,**
**92g cholesterol, 717mg sodium**
**Exchanges: 3 1/2 meat, 3 1/2 starch, 3 1/2 vegetable**

# Green Beans

2 pounds green beans, stems removed

Rinse the beans well, place in a microwave-safe bowl, and cover. Microwave on high for about 4 to 5 minutes until the beans are cooked but not mushy.

**Makes 8 servings, save half for Monday**
**Per serving: 28 calories, 2g protein, 7g carbohydrate, 0 fat,**
**0 cholesterol, 9mg sodium**
**Exchanges: 1 vegetable**

# Meatball Sub Sandwich

4 torpedo rolls

1/2 recipe meatballs and sauce,
  saved from Sunday

Grated Parmesan cheese, optional

Split the rolls in half lengthwise and fill with the meatballs and sauce. Place on a microwave-safe plate, cover with plastic wrap, and microwave on high for a few minutes until heated through. Sprinkle with grated Parmesan cheese, if desired.

**Makes 4 servings**
Per serving: 586 calories, 48g protein, 74g carbohydrate, 8g fat,
92mg cholesterol, 1141mg sodium
Exchanges: 3 1/2 meat, 3 1/2 starch, 3 1/2 vegetable

# Green Bean Vinaigrette

1/2 recipe green beans, saved
  from Sunday

1/2 cup fat-free Italian salad dressing

Toss the green beans with the dressing.

**Makes 4 servings**
Per serving: 29 calories, 1g protein, 7g carbohydrate, 0 fat,
0 cholesterol, 185mg sodium
Exchanges: 1 vegetable

# Minestrone Soup

15-ounce can reduced-sodium
  beef broth

28-ounce can diced tomatoes

16-ounce package frozen Italian-
  style mixed vegetables

10-ounce package frozen chopped
  kale or spinach

14-ounce package frozen white beans

1 1/3 cups soup-mac pasta

1/2 teaspoon garlic powder

1 teaspoon dried thyme

1/4 teaspoon freshly ground black
  pepper

1 tablespoon red wine vinegar

1/2 cup grated Parmesan cheese

In a large saucepan combine all ingredients except the vinegar and
cheese. Bring to a boil, reduce the heat, and simmer for about 8 minutes
or until the pasta is tender. Stir in the vinegar and cheese.

**Makes 4 servings**
**Per serving: 591 calories, 32g protein, 104g carbohydrate, 6g fat,**
**8mg cholesterol, 76mg sodium**
**Exchanges: 2 meat, 5 starch, 3 1/2 vegetable**

Toss the salad while the pizza is cooking.

# Meatball Pizza

10-ounce prepared Italian
  pizza shell

1 cup pizza sauce

8-ounce package Sargento Light
  reduced-fat shredded mozzarella

8 meatballs, saved from Sunday

Preheat the broiler. Place pizza shell on a pizza pan or baking sheet. Spread the sauce over the pizza shell. Sprinkle the cheese over the sauce. Slice the meatballs into 1/4-inch slices and place over the cheese. Cook the pizza under the broiler for a few minutes until heated through and the cheese is browned and melted.

**Makes 4 servings**
**Per serving: 373 calories, 33g protein, 31g carbohydrate, 9g fat,**
**48mg cholesterol, 675mg sodium**
**Exchanges: 3 meat, 2 starch, 1 fat**

# Green Salad

10-ounce bag ready-to-eat salad

1/2 cup fat-free salad dressing

In a large serving bowl, combine the dressing and the salad.

**Makes 4 servings**
**Per serving: 21 calories, 1g protein, 4g carbohydrate, 0 fat,**
**0 cholesterol, 296mg sodium**
**Exchanges: 1 vegetable**

Heat the beans and sauerkraut while the hot dogs are cooking.

# Hot Dog on Roll

14-ounce package Healthy Choice low-fat beef franks

4 hot dog rolls

Mustard, optional

In a medium saucepan, boil the hot dogs in water for a few minutes until heated through. Place two hot dogs in each roll and serve with mustard if desired.

**Makes 4 servings**
**Per serving: 243 calories, 18g protein, 32g carbohydrate, 5g fat,**
**30mg cholesterol, 1101mg sodium**
**Exchanges: 3 meat, 2 starch**

# Baked Beans

16-ounce can fat-free vegetarian-style baked beans

Place the beans in a microwave-safe bowl and cover. Microwave on high for a few minutes or until heated through.

**Makes 4 servings**
**Per serving: 113 calories, 5g protein, 23g carbohydrate, 0 fat,**
**0 cholesterol, 314mg sodium**
**Exchanges: 1 1/2 starch**

# Sauerkraut

14.4-ounce can sauerkraut

Place the sauerkraut in a microwave-safe bowl and cover. Microwave on high for a few minutes or until heated through.

**Makes 4 servings**
**Per serving: 19 calories, 1g protein, 4g carbohydrate, 0 fat,**
**0 cholesterol, 656mg sodium**
**Exchanges: 1 vegetable**

# Pan Bagna

8-inch round loaf good quality
   Italian bread

1/2 cup fat-free Italian salad
   dressing

7-ounce can tuna packed in olive
   oil, drained

7-ounce jar roasted sweet red
   peppers, drained

15-ounce can kidney beans, drained

1 red onion, peeled and sliced

1 ripe tomato, sliced

Cut the bread in half horizontally. Spread half of the salad dressing on the bottom half of the bread. Then layer the tuna, peppers, beans, onion, and tomato. Top with the rest of the salad dressing and the top half of the bread. Cut into 4 wedges.

**Makes 4 servings**
**Per serving: 470 calories, 28g protein, 71g carbohydrate, 8g fat,**
**9mg cholesterol, 1370mg sodium**
**Exchanges: 2 1/2 meat, 3 1/2 starch, 1 1/2 vegetable, 1 fat**

# Week 9

### Sunday

Marinated Chicken Breasts
Roasted Vegetables
Potato Casserole

### Monday

Cream of Potato Soup
Broccoli Slaw

### Tuesday

Chicken, Pasta, and Vegetable Salad

### Wednesday

Ham and Cheese Omelet Sandwich
Stewed Tomatoes

### Thursday

Chicken Ranch Roll-Up Sandwich
Dilled Pea Salad

### Friday

Hawaiian Pizza
Green Salad

# Week 9

## Staples

Bottled favorite fat-free salad dressing
Bottled fat-free ranch salad dressing
Fat-free mayonnaise
Extra virgin olive oil
Balsamic vinegar
Lemon juice
Dijon or grainy-type mustard
Instant low-sodium vegetable or
    chicken broth
Sugar

**Seasonings**
Garlic powder
Crushed thyme
Dried dillweed
Parsley flakes
Salt
Black pepper

# Week 9

## Fresh Produce

3 pounds Yukon Gold potatoes
16-ounce package broccoli slaw
    (shredded broccoli)
10-ounce package ready-to-eat salad
10-ounce package ready-to-eat
    romaine salad
2 ripe tomatoes
1 pound baby carrots
1 red bell pepper
1 bunch asparagus
1 medium zucchini
1 red onion

## Canned and Bottled Foods

Bottled fat-free coleslaw dressing
Small jar mild salsa
7-ounce jar roasted sweet red peppers
28-ounce can stewed tomatoes
8-ounce can crushed pineapple
Small jar pizza sauce
15-ounce can reduced-sodium
    chicken broth

## Breads and Grains

12-ounce package rotini primavera
    pasta
8 slices sandwich bread
12-ounce package lavash bread
    (4 count)
10-ounce prepared Italian pizza shell

## Frozen Foods

16-ounce package peas

## Dairy Foods

Skim milk
Grated Parmesan cheese
8-ounce package Sargento Light
    reduced-fat shredded mozzarella
    cheese
8-ounce package Sargento Light
    reduced-fat shredded cheddar
    cheese
4 slices reduced-fat cheese
16-ounce carton egg substitute

## Meats, Poultry, and Seafood

2 1/2 pounds chicken breasts, boned
    and skinned (10 halves)
8 ounces lean ham

# Week 9

## Sunday

Here are the same recipes for chicken and vegetables from Week One. They are so good that I don't see any need to change them, however, the leftovers are used differently. If you are cooking the chicken under the broiler then cook the potato casserole and vegetables first. The potatoes and vegetables cook at the same temperature and they can hold while the chicken cooks.

## Marinated Chicken Breasts

Note that the chicken breasts need to marinate for several hours in advance of cooking.

1/2 cup vegetable or chicken broth (instant is fine)

1 tablespoon extra virgin olive oil

3 tablespoons balsamic vinegar

2 teaspoons Dijon or grainy-type mustard

2 teaspoons sugar

1/2 teaspoon garlic powder or 1 to 2 minced garlic cloves

1 teaspoon crushed thyme

1/4 teaspoon freshly ground black pepper

Salt to taste, optional

2 1/2 pounds chicken breasts, boned and skinned (10 halves)

Place all ingredients except chicken breasts in a jar with a tight-fitting lid and shake well. Rinse chicken breasts and pat dry with paper towels. Place chicken breasts and marinade in a zipping plastic bag, making sure the chicken is coated well (using a bag saves on cleanup, but a shallow dish covered with plastic wrap works just as well). Marinate the chicken in the refrigerator for several hours, turning occasionally. Prepare outdoor grill or preheat the broiler, or use a stovetop grill pan. Grill the chicken or place under the broiler for about 10 minutes per side. Cooking time will vary depending on the thickness of the chicken. The chicken is done when the internal temperature reaches 165° using an instant-read thermometer. Discard the marinade.

**Makes 10 servings, save three servings for Tuesday, and three servings for Thursday**

Per serving: 164 calories, 25g protein, 3g carbohydrate, 5g fat,
69mg cholesterol, 159mg sodium
Exchanges: 3 meat

# Roasted Vegetables

The vegetables listed here work great but feel free to use whatever vegetables you prefer. Any combination of vegetables will work. Roasting brings out the natural sweetness of vegetables and creates a delicious flavor.

1 pound baby carrots

1 red bell pepper, cored and cut into strips

1 bunch asparagus, ends trimmed and broken into 1-inch pieces

1 medium zucchini, halved and cut into 1-inch pieces

1 teaspoon extra virgin olive oil

Salt to taste, optional

Freshly ground black pepper to taste

Balsamic vinegar to taste

Preheat the oven to 450°. Line two baking pans with foil (makes cleanup easier). Spread the vegetables in a single layer on the foil-lined sheets. Don't overcrowd, or the vegetables will steam instead of roast. You may need to roast the vegetables in two batches. Sprinkle the vegetables with the olive oil or spray with olive oil if you keep your oil in a spray bottle. Roast in the oven for 10 to 15 minutes, stirring once. Transfer the vegetables to a serving bowl and toss with salt, pepper, and vinegar. The vegetables can be served hot, cold, or at room temperature.

Makes 8 servings, save half for Tuesday
Per serving: 50 calories, 2g protein, 10g carbohydrate, 1g fat,
0 cholesterol, 51mg sodium
Exchanges: 2 vegetable

# Potato Casserole

1 teaspoon extra virgin olive oil

3 pounds Yukon Gold potatoes, peeled and thinly sliced

1/8 teaspoon freshly ground black pepper

1 1/2 cups skim milk

7-ounce jar roasted sweet red peppers, drained and chopped

1/4 cup grated Parmesan cheese

1 tablespoon parsley flakes

Preheat the oven to 450°. Coat a large baking pan with the oil. Arrange the sliced potatoes in layers in the baking pan and sprinkle with pepper.

Bake in the oven for 15 minutes. Remove from the oven and pour the milk over the potatoes. Top with the red peppers, cheese, and parsley. Return to the oven and bake another 30 minutes until the potatoes are tender and the top is golden brown.

**Makes 8 servings, save half for Monday**
**Per serving: 219 calories, 7g protein, 46g carbohydrate, 2g fat,**
**3mg cholesterol, 80mg sodium**
**Exchanges: 2 1/2 starch**

# Pasta

12-ounce package rotini primavera

Cook pasta according to package directions. Save for Tuesday.

## Monday

# Cream of Potato Soup

1/2 recipe potato casserole, saved from Sunday

15-ounce can reduced-sodium chicken broth

1 cup skim milk

8-ounce package Sargento Light reduced-fat shredded cheddar cheese

Freshly ground black pepper to taste

In a large saucepan, combine the potatoes, broth, and milk. Bring to a boil, reduce heat, and simmer for several minutes. Mash the potatoes with a potato masher, or use a hand-held blender for a smoother consistency. Remove from the heat and add the cheese and pepper. Stir until the cheese is melted.

**Makes 4 servings**
**Per serving: 390 calories, 26g protein, 50g carbohydrate, 11g fat,**
**25mg cholesterol, 543mg sodium**
**Exchanges: 2 1/2 meat, 2 1/2 starch, 1/2 milk, 1 fat**

# Broccoli Slaw

16-ounce package broccoli slaw
(shredded broccoli)

1/2 cup bottled fat-free coleslaw
dressing

Combine together in a large serving bowl.

**Makes 4 servings**
**Per serving: 52 calories, 3g protein, 10g carbohydrate, 0 fat,**
**0 cholesterol, 241 mg sodium**
**Exchanges: 2 vegetable**

## Tuesday

# Chicken, Pasta, and Vegetable Salad

I make this salad in many variations with additions such as cooked chick-peas, sun-dried tomatoes, reduced-fat shredded cheese, pine nuts, fresh basil, and my own vinaigrette dressing when I have time. It is always a big success at buffets.

3 servings marinated chicken
breasts, saved from Sunday, sliced

1/2 recipe roasted vegetables, saved
from Sunday

Cooked pasta, saved from Sunday

1/2 cup bottled fat-free Italian
salad dressing

Combine all ingredients together in a large serving bowl.

**Makes 4 servings**
**Per serving: 519 calories, 32g protein, 83g carbohydrate, 6g fat,**
**52mg cholesterol, 536mg sodium**
**Exchanges: 2 meat, 3 1/2 starch, 2 vegetable**

# Ham and Cheese Omelet Sandwich

16-ounce carton egg substitute

4 ounces lean ham, chopped

8 slices sandwich bread

4 slices reduced-fat cheese

Heat a large skillet over low heat. Add the egg substitute. Cook over low heat, lifting the edges of the omelet and turning the skillet so the uncooked egg spreads to the bottom of the pan. When the egg is cooked, sprinkle the ham over the top. Fold the omelet in half. Divide the omelet into four sections and place each section on a piece of bread. Top with a slice of cheese and another slice of bread.

**Makes 4 servings**
**Per serving: 290 calories, 29g protein, 32g carbohydrate, 4g fat,**
**24mg cholesterol, 810mg sodium**
**Exchanges: 3 meat, 2 starch**

# Stewed Tomatoes

28-ounce can stewed tomatoes

Heat the tomatoes in a large saucepan or in the microwave in a covered microwave-safe dish.

**Makes 4 servings**
**Per serving: 120 calories, 3g protein, 27g carbohydrate, 0 fat,**
**0 cholesterol, 750mg sodium**
**Exchanges: 5 vegetable**

# Chicken Ranch Roll-Up Sandwich

12-ounce package lavash bread
  (4 count)
1/2 cup fat-free ranch salad
  dressing
1/2 cup mild salsa

3 servings marinated chicken
  breasts, saved from Sunday, sliced
1 red onion, peeled and chopped
10-ounce package ready-to-eat
  romaine salad

Spread 2 tablespoons of salad dressing and salsa on each piece of lavash bread. Divide the chicken, onion, and lettuce equally over the dressing and salsa. Roll up the sandwich.

**Makes 4 servings**
**Per serving: 374 calories, 28g protein, 48g carbohydrate, 8g fat,**
**52mg cholesterol, 849mg sodium**
**Exchanges: 2 meat, 3 starch**

# Dilled Pea Salad

16-ounce package frozen peas
1/3 cup fat-free mayonnaise
1 tablespoon lemon juice

2 teaspoons dried dillweed
Freshly ground black pepper to taste

Defrost the peas in the microwave. Combine all ingredients together in a large serving bowl.

**Makes 4 servings**
**Per serving: 108 calories, 6g protein, 20g carbohydrate, 0 fat,**
**0 cholesterol, 243mg sodium**
**Exchanges: 1 1/2 starch**

# Hawaiian Pizza

10-ounce prepared Italian
  pizza shell
1 cup pizza sauce
8-ounce package Sargento Light
  reduced-fat shredded mozzarella
  cheese

4 ounces lean ham, chopped
8-ounce can crushed pineapple,
  drained

Preheat the broiler. Place the pizza shell on a pizza pan or baking sheet.
Spread the sauce over the shell. Sprinkle the cheese over the sauce.
Sprinkle the ham and pineapple over the cheese. Place the pizza under
the broiler and cook for a few minutes until the pizza is heated through
and the cheese is melted and browned.

**Makes 4 servings**
**Per serving: 367 calories, 29g protein, 35g carbohydrate, 8g fat,**
**38mg cholesterol, 879mg sodium**
**Exchanges: 3 meat, 2 starch, 1/2 vegetable, 1 fat**

# Green Salad

10-ounce package ready-to-eat salad   1/2 cup fat-free salad dressing

Combine together in a large serving bowl.

**Makes 4 servings**
**Per serving: 21 calories, 1g protein, 4g carbohydrate, 0 fat,**
**0 cholesterol, 296mg sodium**
**Exchanges: 1 vegetable**

# Week 10

### Sunday
Roast Turkey Breast with Gravy
Cranberry Sauce
Stuffing
Sweet Potatoes
Green Beans

### Monday
Turkey Waldorf Salad

### Tuesday
Turkey Casserole

### Wednesday
Turkey Reuben Sandwich
Cucumber Salad

### Thursday
Greek Salad with White Beans
Pita Bread

### Friday
Capellini with Clam Sauce
Snow Pea Salad

# Week 10

## Staples

Bottled fat-free Russian salad dressing
Bottled fat-free Greek salad dressing
Bottled fat-free Italian salad dressing
Fat-free mayonnaise
Rice vinegar
Cider vinegar
Lemon juice
Extra virgin olive oil
Canola oil
Cornstarch
Sugar
Raisins
Chopped walnuts

**Seasonings**
Dried dillweed
Garlic powder
Red pepper flakes
Parsley flakes
Crushed thyme
Ground sage
Freshly ground black pepper

# Week 10

**Fresh Produce**

2 pounds green beans

4 sweet potatoes

1 bunch celery

1 onion

2 red onions

3 cucumbers

2 ripe tomatoes

1 green bell pepper

2 10-ounce bags ready-to-eat salad

2 apples

**Canned and Bottled Foods**

8-ounce can cranberry sauce

12-ounce jar fat-free gravy

8-ounce can sauerkraut

10.75-ounce can reduced-fat cream of
   mushroom soup

4-ounce can sliced mushrooms

8-ounce can sliced water chestnuts

7-ounce jar roasted sweet red peppers

19-ounce can white beans

15-ounce can reduced-sodium
   chicken broth

2 6.5-ounce cans chopped clams

13.5-ounce bottle clam juice

Small jar pitted kalamata or Greek-
   style olives

**Breads and Grains**

8-ounce package bow-tie pasta

12-ounce package angel hair pasta

1 pound loaf white bread

8 slices rye bread

4 pita bread rounds

**Frozen Foods**

6-ounce package snow peas

**Dairy Foods**

8 ounces crumbled feta cheese

4 slices reduced-fat Swiss cheese

4-ounce carton egg substitute

**Meats, Poultry, and Seafood**

4-pound boneless turkey breast

# Week 10

## Sunday

I love having turkey leftovers to use during the week. It is so much easier using a boneless breast instead of the whole turkey because you don't have to deal with the carcass. The turkey, stuffing, and potatoes can all cook in the oven at the same time. Start the turkey first since it takes the longest time to cook. To save time during the week, slice the turkey before storing in the refrigerator.

## Roast Turkey Breast

**4-pound boneless turkey breast**

Preheat the oven to 350°. Rinse the turkey and pat dry with paper towels. Place the turkey in a roasting pan and cook in the oven for about 1 1/2 hours (20 to 25 minutes per pound) or until the internal temperature reaches 165° using an instant-read thermometer. Baste several times during cooking. Let rest for 20 minutes before carving. Save the pan drippings for gravy.

**Makes 16 servings, save three-fourths for Monday, Tuesday, and Wednesday**
**Per serving (without skin): 131 calories, 23g protein, 0 carbohydrate, 4g fat,**
**44mg cholesterol, 412mg sodium**
**Exchanges: 3 meat**

## Gravy

Again, a cheat to make gravy.

**Pan drippings**                    **12-ounce jar fat-free gravy**

Pour the pan drippings into a measuring cup with a bottom pour spout. When all the fat comes up to the top of the measuring cup, pour the broth from the bottom back into the pan and discard the fat. Add the jar of gravy and heat over medium-high heat for a few minutes until hot and bubbling.

**Makes 8 servings, save half for Tuesday**
**Per serving: 10 calories, 1g protein, 3g carbohydrate, 0 fat,**
**0 cholesterol, 350mg sodium**
**Exchanges: free food**

# Cranberry Sauce

8-ounce can cranberry sauce

Chill the cranberry sauce in the refrigerator.

**Makes 4 servings**
**Per serving: 78 calories, 0 protein, 20g carbohydrate, 0 fat,**
**0 cholesterol, 15mg sodium**
**Exchanges: 1 fruit**

# Stuffing

1 teaspoon canola oil
1 onion, peeled and chopped
2 stalks celery, chopped
1 pound white bread, torn into
   1-inch pieces
1/2 cup egg substitute

15-ounce can reduced-sodium
   chicken broth
1 tablespoon ground sage
1 teaspoon crushed thyme
1/8 teaspoon freshly ground black
   pepper

Preheat oven to 350°. In a large saucepan, sauté the onion and celery in the canola oil over medium-high heat until the vegetables are wilted. In a large bowl combine the wilted vegetables with the remaining ingredients. Transfer into a large casserole dish, cover, and cook for about an hour.

**Makes 8 servings, save half for Tuesday**
**Per serving: 178 calories, 7g protein, 31g carbohydrate, 3g fat,**
**2mg cholesterol, 356mg sodium**
**Exchanges: 2 starch**

# Sweet Potatoes

4 sweet potatoes

Preheat oven to 350°. Scrub the potatoes and pierce several times with a fork. Bake for about an hour or until the potatoes can easily be pierced with a fork.

**Makes 4 servings**
**Per serving: 117 calories, 2g protein, 28g carbohydrate, 0 fat,**
**0 cholesterol, 11mg sodium**
**Exchanges: 1 1/2 starch**

# Green Beans

2 pounds fresh green beans

Wash and trim the green beans. Place in a microwave-safe dish and cover. Microwave on high for 4 to 5 minutes until the beans are cooked but not mushy.

**Makes 8 servings, save half for Tuesday**
**Per serving: 28 calories, 2g protein, 7g carbohydrate, 0 fat,**
**0 cholesterol, 9mg sodium**
**Exchanges: 1 vegetable**

# Pasta

8 ounces bow-tie pasta

Cook pasta according to package directions. Save for Monday.

## Monday

# Turkey Waldorf Salad

This is a delicious salad and simple to make. It's a nice change from plain old turkey salad.

| | |
|---|---|
| 1/2 cup fat-free mayonnaise | 2 stalks celery, diced |
| 2 tablespoons sugar | 1 red onion, peeled and diced |
| 2 tablespoons cider vinegar | 2 apples, cored and diced |
| 1 teaspoon lemon juice | 1/4 cup raisins |
| 1/4 turkey breast, saved from Sunday, cut into bite-size pieces | 1/2 cup chopped walnuts |
| | Freshly ground black pepper to taste |
| 8 ounces cooked bow-tie pasta, saved from Sunday | 10-ounce package ready-to-eat salad |

In a large serving bowl, whisk together the mayonnaise, sugar, vinegar, and lemon juice. Add the remaining ingredients except the salad and mix together until well combined. Serve over salad.

**Makes 4 servings**
**Per serving: 526 calories, 34g protein, 77g carbohydrate, 9g fat,**
**44mg cholesterol, 650mg sodium**
**Exchanges: 3 meat, 3 starch, 1 vegetable, 1 fruit**

# Turkey Casserole

This casserole can also be assembled ahead of time and cooked in the oven instead of the microwave. I usually heat in the microwave to save time.

1/4 turkey breast, saved from Sunday, sliced

1/2 recipe stuffing, saved from Sunday

1/2 recipe green beans, saved from Sunday

4-ounce can sliced mushrooms, drained

1/2 recipe gravy, saved from Sunday

10.75-ounce can reduced-fat cream of mushroom soup

In a large shallow casserole dish or baking pan, layer the turkey slices, stuffing, green beans, and mushrooms. Mix together the gravy and mushroom soup. Pour the soup mixture over the other ingredients in the casserole dish. Cover with plastic wrap and microwave on high for several minutes or until heated through.

**Makes 4 servings**
**Per serving: 411 calories, 34g protein, 48g carbohydrate, 10g fat,**
**50mg cholesterol, 1384mg sodium**
**Exchanges: 3 meat, 2 starch, 1 1/2 vegetable, 1 fat**

# Turkey Reuben Sandwich

8 slices rye bread

1/4 turkey breast, saved from
Sunday, sliced

4 slices reduced-fat Swiss cheese

1/2 cup fat-free Russian salad dressing

8-ounce can sauerkraut, drained

On each of four slices of bread, divide the turkey, cheese, salad dressing, and sauerkraut. Top with the remaining slices of bread. Place the sandwiches in the microwave for a couple minutes on high until the cheese is melted.

**Makes 4 servings**
Per serving: 379 calories, 37g protein, 40g carbohydrate, 7g fat,
54mg cholesterol, 1457mg sodium
Exchanges: 4 meat, 2 1/2 starch, 1/2 vegetable

# Cucumber Salad

2 cucumbers, peeled and sliced thin    1/2 cup fat-free Italian salad dressing

In a large serving bowl, combine the cucumbers and dressing.

**Makes 4 servings**
Per serving: 50 calories, 1g protein, 11g carbohydrate, 0 fat,
0 cholesterol, 363mg sodium
Exchanges: 2 vegetable

# Greek Salad with White Beans and Pita Bread

10-ounce package ready-to-eat salad

2 ripe tomatoes, sliced

1 cucumber, peeled and sliced

1 red onion, peeled and sliced

19-ounce can white beans, drained

4 ounces crumbled feta cheese

1/2 cup pitted kalamata or Greek-style olives

1/2 cup fat-free Greek salad dressing

4 pita bread rounds

In a large serving bowl, combine all the ingredients except the pita bread and mix well. Serve with pita bread.

Makes 4 servings
Per serving: 354 calories, 18g protein, 50g carbohydrate, 10g fat,
25mg cholesterol, 1114mg sodium
Exchanges: 2 meat, 3 starch, 1 1/2 vegetable, 1 fat

# Capellini with Clam Sauce

This is a quick but delicious clam sauce. I let people
add their own red pepper flakes at the table.

12-ounce package angel hair pasta

2 6.5-ounce cans chopped clams,
   drained

13.5-ounce bottle clam juice

1 tablespoon lemon juice

1/2 teaspoon garlic powder

2 tablespoons parsley flakes

Red pepper flakes to taste

1 tablespoon cornstarch mixed
   with 3 tablespoons water

Boil the pasta in 2 quarts of water for 2 to 3 minutes and drain. While the
pasta is cooking, heat the clams, clam juice, lemon juice, and seasonings
in a medium saucepan. Add the cornstarch and water to the clam sauce
and continue to heat and stir until the sauce thickens. Combine the
sauce with the pasta.

Makes 4 servings
Per serving: 355 calories, 17g protein, 67g carbohydrate, 1g fat,
0 cholesterol, 731mg sodium
Exchanges: 1 meat, 3 starch

# Snow Pea Salad

6-ounce package frozen snow peas

8-ounce can sliced water chestnuts,
   drained

7-ounce jar roasted sweet red
   peppers, drained and chopped

1/4 cup rice vinegar

Defrost the snow peas in the microwave. In a medium serving bowl,
combine the snow peas, water chestnuts, peppers, and vinegar.

Makes 4 servings.
Per serving: 44 calories, 1g protein, 8g carbohydrate, 0 fat,
0 cholesterol, 8mg sodium
Exchanges: 1 1/2 vegetable

# Week 11

### Sunday
Marinated Grilled Beef
Brown Rice
Broccoli

### Monday
Oriental Beef Salad

### Tuesday
Sweet and Sour Beef and Vegetables
   with Rice

### Wednesday
Veggie Pizza Pasta

### Thursday
Antipasto Salad
Italian Bread

### Friday
Seafood Salad Roll-Up Sandwich
Three-Bean Salad

# Week 11

## Staples

Bottled fat-free mayonnaise
Bottled fat-free Italian salad dressing
Soy sauce
Rice vinegar
Sherry or cooking sherry
Lemon juice
Sugar

**Seasonings**
Ground ginger
Crushed oregano

# Week 11

**Fresh Produce**

2 1/4 pounds broccoli

10-ounce package ready-to-eat Italian salad blend

10-ounce package ready-to-eat green salad

1 cucumber

3 ripe tomatoes

2 cloves garlic (or use bottled)

1 celery stalk

**Canned and Bottled Foods**

15-ounce can mandarin oranges, packed in juice

20-ounce can chunk pineapple, packed in juice

15-ounce can baby corn

14-ounce can artichoke hearts, not packed in oil

7-ounce jar roasted sweet red peppers

2 6-ounce cans tuna, packed in olive oil

15.5-ounce can chick-peas

16-ounce jar three-bean salad

2.25-ounce can sliced black olives

26-ounce jar Healthy Choice primavera pasta sauce

Bottled fat-free Oriental mandarin dressing

Bottled hoisin sauce

Bottled Oriental sweet and sour sauce

**Breads and Grains**

16-ounce package brown rice

12-ounce package rotelle pasta

1/2 pound loaf Italian bread

12-ounce package lavash bread (4 count)

8-ounce package rice sticks (cellophane noodles)

**Frozen Foods**

6-ounce package snow peas

16-ounce package sugar-snap mix stir-fry vegetables

**Dairy Foods**

8-ounce package Sargento Light reduced-fat shredded mozzarella cheese

**Meats, Poultry, and Seafood**

3 pounds lean steak such as flank steak

12 ounces cooked crabmeat or imitation seafood salad

# Week 11

## Marinated Grilled Beef

Marinating and slicing thinly across the grain makes this very tender and provides a wonderful flavor. Note the steak needs to marinate for several hours in advance of cooking.

6 tablespoons soy sauce

2 tablespoons hoisin sauce

1/4 cup sherry or cooking sherry

1 tablespoon rice vinegar

2 tablespoons sugar

2 cloves garlic, peeled and minced (bottled is fine)

1/4 teaspoon ground ginger

3 pounds lean steak such as flank steak

Combine all ingredients except the steak in a jar with a lid and shake well. Rinse the steak and pat dry with paper towels. Place the steak in a large zipping bag, add the marinade, and gently shake the bag to make sure the steak is well coated with the marinade. You can also use a large shallow dish but a bag saves on cleanup. Marinate for several hours in the refrigerator. Prepare the outdoor grill, or preheat the broiler. Grill the steak or place under the broiler for about 10 minutes per side, depending on thickness. Let the steak rest for several minutes, then slice very thinly across the grain.

**Makes 12 servings, save one-third for Monday and one-third for Tuesday**
**Per serving: 217 calories, 28g protein, 3g carbohydrate, 9g fat,**
**47mg cholesterol, 601mg sodium**
**Exchanges: 3 meat**

# Brown Rice

16-ounce package brown rice          6 cups water

In a large saucepan combine the rice and water. Bring to a boil, cover, and simmer for about 45 minutes or until the water is absorbed and the rice is tender.

**Makes 8 servings, save half for Tuesday**
**Per serving: 213 calories, 5g protein, 46g carbohydrate, 2g fat,**
**0 cholesterol, 0 sodium**
**Exchanges: 3 starch**

# Broccoli

2 1/4 pounds fresh broccoli

Wash the broccoli and cut into small florets. The stems can be peeled and sliced. Place florets and stems in a microwave-safe bowl, cover, and microwave on high for 4 to 5 minutes. The broccoli should be tender but not mushy.

**Makes 8 servings, save half for Wednesday**
**Per serving: 25 calories, 3g protein, 5g carbohydrate, 0 fat,**
**0 cholesterol, 23mg sodium**
**Exchanges: 1 vegetable**

# Rotelle

12-ounce package rotelle pasta

Cook pasta according to package directions. Save for Wednesday.

# Oriental Beef Salad

This is a delicious salad. If you have time you can arrange it attractively on a large platter or individual plates. I never have time to do that but it tastes just as good.

8-ounce package Oriental rice
  sticks (cellophane noodles)
6-ounce package frozen snow peas
10-ounce package ready-to-eat
  green salad
1/3 recipe sliced marinated grilled
  beef, saved from Sunday

1 cucumber, peeled and sliced
15-ounce can mandarin oranges
  packed in fruit juice, drained
1/2 cup bottled fat-free Oriental
  mandarin orange dressing

Boil the rice sticks in 2 quarts of boiling water for 2 to 3 minutes. Place the snow peas in a colander. When the rice sticks are done, drain them in the colander with the snow peas. In a large serving bowl or platter combine all the ingredients.

**Makes 4 servings**
**Per serving: 552 calories, 31g protein, 83g carbohydrate, 9g fat,**
**47mg cholesterol, 774mg sodium**
**Exchanges: 3 meat, 4 starch, 1 vegetable, 1/2 fruit**

# Sweet and Sour Beef and Vegetables with Rice

16-ounce package frozen sugar-snap mix stir-fry vegetables

20-ounce can pineapple chunks packed in fruit juice, drained

1/3 recipe sliced marinated grilled beef, saved from Sunday

1 cup bottled Oriental sweet and sour sauce

1/2 recipe brown rice, saved from Sunday

Place the vegetables in a large nonstick skillet, cover, and cook over high heat for a few minutes until defrosted. Add the pineapple, beef, and sweet and sour sauce. Bring to a boil, reduce heat, and simmer for a minute or until everything is heated through. Place the rice in a microwave-safe dish, cover, and reheat in the microwave on high for a few minutes or until hot. Serve the sweet and sour beef and vegetables over the rice.

**Makes 4 servings**
**Per serving: 677 calories, 36g protein, 108g carbohydrate, 11g fat,**
**47mg cholesterol, 964mg sodium**
**Exchanges: 3 meat, 3 starch, 2 vegetable, 1 1/2 fruit**

# Veggie Pizza Pasta

Kids will love this just because you call it pizza pasta.

Cooked rotelle pasta, saved from
 Sunday
1/2 recipe broccoli, saved from
 Sunday
26-ounce jar Healthy Choice
 primavera pasta sauce

1 teaspoon crushed oregano
8-ounce package Sargento Light
 reduced-fat shredded mozzarella
 cheese

Combine the pasta, broccoli, pasta sauce, and oregano in a large nonstick skillet and heat over high heat. Reduce the heat to low and simmer for a few minutes until heated through. Remove from the heat and stir in the cheese.

**Makes 4 servings**
Per serving: 562 calories, 33g protein, 85g carbohydrate, 8g fat,
20mg cholesterol, 931mg sodium
Exchanges: 2 meat, 3 starch, 4 vegetable

# Antipasto Salad

10-ounce package ready-to-eat
   Italian salad blend

2 ripe tomatoes, sliced

15-ounce can baby corn, drained

14-ounce can artichoke hearts,
   not packed in oil, drained and
   quartered

7-ounce jar roasted sweet red
   peppers, drained and sliced

15.5-ounce can chick-peas, drained

2.25-ounce can sliced black olives,
   drained

2 6-ounce cans tuna packed in
   olive oil, drained

1/2 cup bottled fat-free Italian salad
   dressing

Combine all ingredients in a large serving bowl or platter.

**Makes 4 servings**
**Per serving: 400 calories, 34g protein, 46g carbohydrate, 10g fat,**
**15mg cholesterol, 1140mg sodium**
**Exchanges: 3 1/2 meat, 1 starch, 1 vegetable**

# Italian Bread

1/2 pound Italian bread

**Makes 4 servings**
**Per serving: 154 calories, 5g protein, 28g carbohydrate, 2g fat,**
**0 cholesterol, 331mg sodium**
**Exchanges: 2 starch**

## Seafood Salad Roll-Up Sandwich

12 ounces cooked crabmeat or
   imitation seafood

1/3 cup fat-free mayonnaise

1 tablespoon lemon juice

1 ripe tomato, chopped

1 stalk celery, chopped

12-ounce package lavash bread
   (4 count)

In a large bowl combine the crabmeat or seafood, mayonnaise, lemon juice, tomato, and celery. Spread equally over the 4 slices of bread and roll each into a sandwich.

Makes 4 servings
Per serving: 341 calories, 23g protein, 53g carbohydrate, 3g fat,
85mg cholesterol, 1031mg sodium
Exchanges: 2 meat, 3 starch

## Three-Bean Salad

16-ounce jar three-bean salad

Makes 4 servings
Per serving: 125 calories, 3g protein, 28g carbohydrate, 1g fat,
0 cholesterol, 150mg sodium
Exchanges: 1 starch, 1 vegetable

# Week 12

### Sunday
Eggplant Parmesan
Garlic Green Beans
Ziti

### Monday
Eggplant Parmesan Sandwich
Green Bean Vinaigrette

### Tuesday
Greek Pasta

### Wednesday
Roast Beef Sandwich with
   Horseradish Sauce
Green Salad

### Thursday
Egg Drop Soup
Ramen Noodles

### Friday
Paella Couscous

# Week 12

## Staples

Bread crumbs
Grated Parmesan cheese
Extra virgin olive oil
Lemon juice
Dijon or grainy-type mustard
Fat-free mayonnaise
Bottled fat-free Italian salad dressing
Bottled favorite fat-free salad dressing
Soy sauce
Cornstarch

### Seasonings
Black pepper
Crushed oregano
Garlic powder
Ground ginger
Dried basil

# Week 12

## Fresh Produce

2 1/2 pounds eggplant
2 pounds green beans
10-ounce package ready-to-eat salad
1 onion
1 carrot
2 ripe tomatoes
2 6-ounce packages ready-to-eat baby
    spinach
8 cloves garlic (or use bottled)

## Canned and Bottled Foods

2 28-ounce cans crushed tomatoes
15-ounce can diced tomatoes
6-ounce can tomato paste
2 15-ounce cans reduced-sodium
    chicken broth
2.25-ounce can sliced black olives
Small bottle pitted kalamata or
    Greek-style olives
7-ounce jar roasted sweet red peppers
Small bottle white horseradish

## Breads and Grains

4 torpedo rolls
8 slices whole-grain bread
3 3-ounce packages reduced-fat ramen
    noodles
1-pound package ziti
5.7-ounce package Near East herbed
    chicken-flavor couscous

## Frozen Foods

14-ounce package white beans
14-ounce package chick-peas
10-ounce package peas
16-ounce package mixed stir-fry veg-
    etables

## Dairy Foods

2 8-ounce packages Sargento Light
    reduced-fat shredded mozzarella
    cheese
4 ounces crumbled feta cheese
16-ounce and 4-ounce cartons egg
    substitute

## Meats, Poultry, and Seafood

4 ounces lean ham
12 ounces lean sliced roast beef
4 ounces cooked and peeled shrimp

# Week 12

The green beans and ziti can be prepared while the eggplant bakes.

## Eggplant Parmesan

This is a delicious eggplant Parmesan, and it has much less fat and calories than traditional fried eggplant. The sauce for this recipe is the same used for spaghetti and meatballs in Week Eight. The sauce can simmer while you prepare the eggplant. You may want to reserve a cup or so of the sauce to serve over the ziti and eggplant Parmesan.

### Sauce

1 teaspoon extra virgin olive oil

1 onion, peeled and minced

1 carrot, peeled and minced

4 cloves garlic, peeled and minced
  (bottled is fine)

2 28-ounce cans crushed tomatoes

6-ounce can tomato paste

1 tablespoon crushed oregano

1 teaspoon dried basil

Freshly ground black pepper to taste

In a large nonstick skillet, sauté the onion, carrot, and garlic in the olive oil over medium-high heat until the vegetables are slightly browned and wilted. Add the crushed tomatoes, tomato paste, and seasonings. Bring to a boil, reduce the heat, and simmer uncovered for about 15 minutes.

### Eggplant

2 1/2 pounds eggplant

1/2 cup egg substitute

1 cup bread crumbs

1 teaspoon extra virgin olive oil

Preheat the broiler. Peel the eggplants and slice crosswise into 3/8-inch slices. Place the egg substitute and bread crumbs into shallow bowls or pie plates. Dip the eggplant slices first into the egg then the bread crumbs. Place the coated eggplant slices in a single layer on a cookie sheet or shallow baking pan (you may need more than one pan). Spray or drizzle with half the olive oil. Place under the broiler for a few minutes or until golden brown (watch carefully so it doesn't burn). Turn the slices over and spray or drizzle the other side with olive oil. Again place under the broiler until golden brown.

## Casserole

| | |
|---|---|
| Eggplant from above | 2 8-ounce packages Sargento Light |
| Sauce from above | reduced-fat shredded mozzarella |
| | cheese |
| | 1 cup grated Parmesan cheese |

Preheat the oven to 350°. Place half the eggplant in a large baking pan; cover with half the sauce and half the mozzarella cheese. Repeat to make a second layer using the rest of the eggplant, sauce, and mozzarella cheese. Sprinkle the Parmesan cheese over the top. Bake in the oven for about 30 minutes or until bubbly and browned.

**Makes 8 servings, save half for Monday**
**Per serving: 386 calories, 30g protein, 40g carbohydrate, 11g fat,**
**28mg cholesterol, 1120mg sodium**
**Exchanges: 3 meat, 1 starch, 4 vegetable**

# Garlic Green Beans

| | |
|---|---|
| 1 teaspoon extra virgin olive oil | 2 pounds fresh green beans, |
| 4 cloves garlic, peeled and minced | washed and trimmed |
| (bottled is fine) | 1 tablespoon lemon juice or to taste |

In a large nonstick skillet, sauté the garlic in the olive oil over low heat until wilted. Add the green beans; cover and continue to cook over low heat for about 5 minutes or until the green beans are cooked but not mushy. Stir in the lemon juice.

**Makes 8 servings, save half for Monday**
**Per serving: 33 calories, 2g protein, 7g carbohydrate, 1g fat, 0 cholesterol, 9mg sodium**
**Exchanges: 1 vegetable**

# Ziti

1-pound package ziti

Cook ziti according to package directions.

**Makes 8 servings, save one-half for Tuesday**
**Per serving: 213 calories, 7g protein, 43g carbohydrate, 1g fat, 0 cholesterol, 0 sodium**
**Exchanges: 2 1/2 starch**

# Eggplant Parmesan Sandwich

1/2 recipe eggplant Parmesan,     4 torpedo rolls
  saved from Sunday

Place the eggplant in a microwave-safe dish and cover. Cook in the microwave on high for a few minutes or until heated through. Divide the eggplant into the 4 rolls.

Makes 4 servings
Per serving: 629 calories, 37g protein, 83g carbohydrate, 15g fat,
28mg cholesterol, 1596mg sodium
Exchanges: 3 meat, 4 starch, 4 vegetable

# Green Bean Vinaigrette

1/2 recipe garlic green beans,    1/2 cup fat-free Italian salad
  saved from Sunday        dressing

In a large serving bowl, combine the green beans with the dressing.

Makes 4 servings
Per serving: 48 calories, 2g protein, 10g carbohydrate, 1g fat,
0 cholesterol, 189mg sodium
Exchanges: 2 vegetable

# Greek Pasta

1 teaspoon extra virgin olive oil

2 6-ounce packages ready-to-eat
  baby spinach

14-ounce package frozen white
  beans

15-ounce can diced tomatoes

1/2 recipe cooked ziti, saved
  from Sunday

1/2 cup pitted kalamata or
  Greek-style olives

1 tablespoon crushed oregano

1/2 teaspoon garlic powder

Freshly ground black pepper
  to taste

4 ounces crumbled feta cheese

In a large nonstick skillet, sauté the spinach in the olive oil over high heat for a minute or until the spinach is starting to wilt. Add the beans, tomatoes, ziti, olives, and seasonings. Continue to heat for several minutes, stirring occasionally, until heated through. Remove the pan from the heat and stir in the feta cheese.

**Makes 4 servings**
Per serving: 494 calories, 23g protein, 74g carbohydrate, 11g fat,
25mg cholesterol, 772mg sodium
Exchanges: 2 meat, 4 starch, 1 vegetable, 1 fat

# Roast Beef Sandwich with Horseradish Sauce

1/2 cup fat-free mayonnaise

1 tablespoon white horseradish

1 tablespoon Dijon or grainy-type mustard

12 ounces sliced lean roast beef

2 ripe tomatoes, sliced

8 slices whole-grain bread

Make the horseradish sauce by combining the mayonnaise, horseradish, and mustard in a small bowl. Divide the roast beef, tomatoes, and sauce over 4 slices of bread and top with the remaining 4 slices of bread.

**Makes 4 servings**
**Per serving: 330 calories, 30g protein, 30g carbohydrate, 9g fat,**
**69mg cholesterol, 568mg sodium**
**Exchanges: 3 meat, 2 starch**

# Green Salad

10-ounce package ready-to-eat salad

1/2 cup favorite fat-free salad dressing

In a large serving bowl combine the salad with the dressing.

**Makes 4 servings**
**Per serving: 21 calories, 1g protein, 4g carbohydrate, 0 fat,**
**0 cholesterol, 296mg sodium**
**Exchanges: 1 vegetable**

# Egg Drop Soup

You can add any vegetables to this soup in place of stir-fry vegetables. Spinach and Chinese cabbage are nice additions.

2 15-ounce cans reduced-sodium chicken broth

16-ounce package frozen mixed stir-fry vegetables

1/2 teaspoon garlic powder

1/4 teaspoon ground ginger

3 tablespoons soy sauce

1 tablespoon cornstarch

16-ounce carton egg substitute

In a large saucepan, combine the broth, vegetables, garlic powder, and ginger. Bring to a boil. Stir together the soy sauce and cornstarch in a small bowl. To slightly thicken the soup add the soy sauce mixture to the pan, stirring continuously. While the soup is swirling, slowly add the egg substitute. Remove from the heat.

**Makes 4 servings**
**Per serving: 142 calories, 22g protein, 12g carbohydrate, 0 fat,**
**0 cholesterol, 1130mg sodium**
**Exchanges: 2 meat, 1 1/2 vegetable**

# Ramen Noodles

3 3-ounce packages reduced-fat ramen noodles

Cook noodles according to package directions.

**Makes 4 servings**
**Per serving: 330 calories, 11g protein, 68g carbohydrate, 2g fat,**
**0 cholesterol, 2145mg sodium**
**Exchanges: 4 1/2 starch**

# Paella Couscous

1 1/4 cups water

10-ounce package frozen peas

14-ounce package frozen chick-peas

5.7-ounce package Near East
   herbed chicken-flavor couscous

4 ounces lean ham, cut into
   bite-size pieces

4 ounces peeled and cooked shrimp

7-ounce jar roasted sweet red
   peppers, drained and chopped

2.25-ounce can sliced black olives,
   drained

1 teaspoon extra virgin olive oil

1 tablespoon lemon juice

In a large saucepan combine the water, peas, and chick-peas. Bring to a boil; stir in the couscous with the flavor packet. Remove from heat, cover, and let stand for 5 minutes. Stir in the remaining ingredients.

Makes 4 servings
Per serving: 451 calories, 28g protein, 10g carbohydrate, 7g fat,
69mg cholesterol, 965mg sodium
Exchanges: 3 meat, 4 starch, 1 vegetable

# Quick Pasta Meals

By keeping a well-stocked kitchen you can prepare a quick pasta meal at any time. Here are the items I like to keep stocked in my kitchen just for quick pasta meals:

♦ A variety of types of pastas. I especially like angel hair pasta because it cooks in only 2 to 3 minutes.

♦ Low-fat bottled sauces.

♦ Assorted canned tomatoes—crushed, stewed, diced, seasoned, and tomato paste.

♦ Packaged sun-dried tomatoes.

♦ Seafood—canned chopped clams, tuna, anchovies, and salmon; bottled clam juice; and frozen cooked shrimp.

♦ Frozen and canned beans—chick-peas, kidney beans, and white beans.

♦ Canned and bottled vegetables such as corn, mushrooms, green and black olives, capers, and roasted sweet red peppers.

♦ Frozen vegetables—including chopped spinach, chopped broccoli, onions, peppers, peas, and mixed vegetables.

♦ Peanut butter for Szechuan pasta.

♦ Canned evaporated skim milk for cream sauces.

♦ Parmesan cheese and shredded reduced-fat cheese can be kept in the freezer.

♦ Seasonings—olive oil, vinegars, lemon juice, soy sauce, garlic powder, crushed oregano, dried basil, and freshly ground black pepper.

It seems the longest part about cooking pasta is waiting for the water to boil. I have found that 8 to 12 ounces of pasta will quick perfectly well in 2 quarts of water. This is less than recommended, but really works just fine. The water boils most quickly when the pan is covered and set over high heat. By doing this, I can have boiling water in 7 to 8 minutes. I count on 2 to 3 ounces of pasta per person (8 to 12 ounces for 4 servings).

In addition to the recipes in this chapter, also try Szechuan Peanut Noodles on page 43, Capellini Carbonara on page 94, and Capellini with Clam Sauce on page 124.

# Pasta with Piquant Sauce

This is a great sauce if you like strong, piquant flavors. This pasta goes well with grilled chicken or fish and a green salad.

| | |
|---|---|
| 12 ounces pasta | 1/4 cup green olives, chopped |
| 1 teaspoon extra virgin olive oil | 2 ripe tomatoes, chopped |
| 2 cloves garlic, peeled and minced (bottled is fine) | 1 teaspoon dried basil |
| | Salt to taste |
| 2 anchovy fillets | Red pepper flakes to taste |
| 2 tablespoons capers | |

Cook pasta according to package directions, and drain. While the pasta is cooking, sauté the garlic in the oil in a large skillet over medium-high heat until it is wilted. Add the remaining ingredients, and simmer for a few minutes until heated through. In a large serving bowl or platter, combine the cooked pasta with the sauce.

Makes 4 servings
Per serving: 350 calories, 12g protein, 68g carbohydrate, 3g fat,
2mg cholesterol, 387mg sodium
Exchanges: 3 starch, 1 vegetable

# Pasta with Tomato–Lemon Sauce

This a great sauce to make in the summer when fresh tomatoes are at their peak. You can also add some fresh basil. To round out the meal, try a green salad and some grilled chicken or fish or fresh mozzarella cheese.

12 ounces pasta

4 large ripe tomatoes, diced

2 tablespoons lemon juice

1 teaspoon extra virgin olive oil

Salt to taste

Freshly ground black pepper to taste

Boil pasta according to package directions, and drain. In a large serving bowl or platter, combine the cooked pasta with the remaining ingredients.

**Makes 4 servings**
**Per serving: 375 calories, 13g protein, 74g carbohydrate, 3g fat,**
**0 cholesterol, 26mg sodium**
**Exchanges: 3 starch, 2 vegetable**


# Pasta with Seafood Sauce

To round out the meal, serve with a green salad.

12 ounces pasta

1 teaspoon extra virgin olive oil

2 cloves garlic, peeled and minced
   (bottled is fine)

28-ounce can crushed tomatoes

12 ounces cooked and peeled shrimp
   or other seafood

1 teaspoon crushed oregano

1 teaspoon dried basil

Salt to taste

Freshly ground black pepper to
   taste

Cook pasta according to package directions, and drain. While the pasta is cooking, sauté the garlic in the oil in a large skillet over medium-high heat until wilted. Add the remaining ingredients, and simmer for a few minutes until heated through. In a large serving bowl or platter, combine the cooked pasta with the sauce.

**Makes 4 servings**
**Per serving: 471 calories, 32g protein, 76g carbohydrate, 4g fat,**
**166mg cholesterol, 646mg sodium**
**Exchanges: 3 meat, 3 starch, 2 vegetable**

# Pasta with Greens

This is very good served with grilled chicken or fish.

12 ounces pasta

1 pound fresh arugula or spinach, washed well (or use ready-to-eat)

26-ounce jar low-fat pasta sauce

Grated Parmesan cheese, optional

Cook pasta according to package directions, adding greens during the last few minutes of cooking. Drain pasta and greens. In a large serving bowl or platter, combine the cooked pasta and greens with the sauce. Serve with Parmesan cheese if desired.

**Makes 4 servings**
**Per serving: 406 calories, 16g protein, 79g carbohydrate, 3g fat,**
**0 cholesterol, 517mg sodium**
**Exchanges: 3 starch, 3 vegetable**

# Pasta with Pesto Sauce

This is a great sauce to make in the summer when basil is plentiful. It's about the only time I use my food processor. This pasta also goes well with grilled chicken or fish.

12 ounces pasta

1 1/2 cups fresh basil leaves

2 to 4 cloves garlic, peeled

1/4 cup pine nuts or walnuts

1/4 cup grated Parmesan cheese

2 tablespoons lemon juice

2 tablespoons vegetable broth or more if needed

1 tablespoon extra virgin olive oil

Cook pasta according to package directions, and drain. While the pasta is cooking, add the remaining ingredients to the food processor and purée until smooth, adding more broth if needed for a smooth consistency. In a large serving bowl or platter, combine the cooked pasta with the sauce.

**Makes 4 servings**
**Per serving: 423 calories, 15g protein, 66g carbohydrate, 11g fat,**
**4mg cholesterol, 100mg sodium**
**Exchanges: 3 starch, 2 fat**

# Pasta Primavera Alfredo

To boost the protein in this dish, add some cooked chicken, fish, or beans.
You can also use a jar of low-fat pasta sauce instead of making an alfredo sauce.

12 ounces pasta

16-ounce package frozen mixed
  vegetables

12-ounce can evaporated skim milk

1 teaspoon garlic powder

Salt to taste

Freshly ground black pepper to taste

2 tablespoons cornstarch mixed
  with 2 tablespoons water

1/2 cup grated Parmesan cheese

Cook pasta according to package directions. Place the vegetables in a colander, and place the colander over the boiling pasta to steam the vegetables while the pasta cooks. Drain the pasta in the colander with the vegetables. While the pasta drains, heat the milk and the seasonings. Add the cornstarch mixture, and continue to heat until the milk thickens. In a large serving bowl or platter, combine the cooked pasta and vegetables with the sauce. Sprinkle the top with Parmesan cheese.

**Makes 4 servings**
**Per serving: 524 calories, 25g protein, 95g carbohydrate, 5g fat,**
**11mg cholesterol, 338mg sodium**
**Exchanges: 3 starch, 2 vegetables, 1 milk**

Casseroles are great to make ahead of time to be ready when company is coming or if you need something for the babysitter to put in the oven.

# Stuffed Shells Florentine

12-ounce package jumbo shells

1/2 cup egg substitute

1/2 cup grated Parmesan cheese

32 ounces fat-free ricotta cheese

16 ounces frozen chopped spinach, thawed

3 ounces sun-dried tomatoes, plumped in hot water, drained and chopped

2 26-ounce jars Healthy Choice pasta sauce

8-ounce package Sargento Light reduced-fat shredded Italian blend cheese

Cook shells according to package directions and drain. In a large bowl mix together the egg substitute, Parmesan cheese, ricotta cheese, spinach, and tomatoes. Stuff the shells with the cheese mixture and place in a 9 x 13 inch casserole pan. Pour the sauce over the shells and sprinkle with the shredded cheese. Bake in a preheated 350° oven for 40 minutes covered and 10 minutes uncovered. Add 10 minutes cooking time if casserole was made ahead and stored in the refrigerator.

**Makes 10 servings**
**Per serving: 348 calories, 30g protein, 46g carbohydrate, 5g fat,**
**19mg cholesterol, 897mg sodium**
**Exchanges: 3 meat, 2 starch, 2 vegetable**

# Sweet and Sour Unstuffed Cabbage

This tastes like the delicious stuffed cabbage my grandmother used to make but without all the work of rolling cabbage leaves.

1 pound ground turkey breast or
   95% lean ground beef

1 large onion, peeled and chopped

2 pounds cabbage, cored and
   shredded

8-ounce can tomato sauce

28-ounce can crushed tomatoes

1/4 cup sugar

1/4 cup lemon juice

1/2 cup raisins

1 cup white rice, uncooked

Preheat oven to 350°. Combine all ingredients in a large 9 x 13 inch casserole pan. Cover and bake for 2 hours. Increase cooking time by 10 to 15 minutes if the casserole was made ahead and stored in the refrigerator.

**Makes 4 servings**
**Per serving: 485 calories, 34g protein, 80g carbohydrate, 4g fat,**
**69mg cholesterol, 902mg sodium**
**Exchanges: 3 meat, 2 starch, 4 vegetable**

# Baked Macaroni and Cheese

This recipe is easily doubled for a larger crowd.

8 ounces elbow macaroni

2 cups skim milk

2 tablespoons cornstarch

8 ounces Sargento Light reduced-
   fat shredded cheddar cheese

Dash Worcestershire sauce

1/2 cup bread crumbs

1/2 cup grated Parmesan cheese

Cook pasta according to package directions and drain. In a large saucepan combine the milk and cornstarch; heat over medium heat, continually stirring. When the milk has thickened, remove from the heat and add the cheese and Worcestershire sauce. Continue stirring until the cheese melts. Mix the macaroni and cheese together and place in a small casserole pan. Sprinkle the top with bread crumbs and Parmesan cheese. Bake in a preheated 375° oven for 40 minutes, increasing cooking time by 10 minutes if the casserole was made ahead and stored in the refrigerator.

**Makes 4 servings**
**Per serving: 508 calories, 33g protein, 63g carbohydrate, 12g fat,**
**30mg cholesterol, 725mg sodium**
**Exchanges: 3 meat, 3 1/2 starch, 1 fat**

# Mexican Lasagna

11.5-ounce package fat-free tortillas

19-ounce can black beans, drained

15.25-ounce can kernel corn, drained

1 green bell pepper, cored and chopped

16-ounce jar salsa

8-ounce package Sargento Light reduced-fat shredded Mexican blend cheese

Chopped lettuce, optional

Chopped tomato, optional

Fat-free sour cream, optional

Preheat oven to 375°. In a large 9 x 13 inch casserole pan place a layer of half of the tortillas. On top of the tortillas spread half the beans, corn, pepper, salsa, and cheese. Repeat the layers, ending with cheese. Cover the casserole and bake for 30 minutes, increasing cooking time by 10 minutes if the casserole was made ahead and stored in the refrigerator. Uncover and cook for another 10 minutes. Garnish with lettuce, tomato, and sour cream if desired.

**Makes 6 servings**
**Per serving: 317 calories, 21g protein, 46g carbohydrate, 5g fat,**
**14mg cholesterol, 1268mg sodium**
**Exchanges: 2 meat, 3 starch**

# Vegetable Lasagna

10-ounce package frozen chopped spinach, thawed and drained

16 ounces fat-free ricotta cheese

8-ounce package Sargento Light reduced-fat shredded mozzarella cheese

1/2 cup grated Parmesan cheese

1/4 cup egg substitute

7-ounce jar roasted sweet red peppers, drained and chopped

26-ounce jar Healthy Choice pasta sauce

8-ounce package oven-ready lasagna noodles

Preheat oven to 350°. In a large bowl combine the spinach, ricotta cheese, mozzarella cheese, Parmesan cheese, egg substitute, and peppers. Spread 1/2 cup of pasta sauce in the bottom of a 9 x 13 inch casserole pan. Arrange a layer of lasagna noodles over the sauce and spread half of the cheese mixture over the noodles. Pour 1 cup of pasta sauce over the cheese mixture. Repeat the layers, ending with a layer of lasagna noodles topped with 1/2 cup of pasta sauce. Cover the pan and bake in a for 30 minutes, adding 10 minutes if lasagna was made ahead and stored in the refrigerator. Uncover the pan and cook for another 15 minutes.

**Makes 6 servings**
**Per serving: 374 calories, 28g protein, 45g carbohydrate, 8g fat,**
**32mg cholesterol, 857mg sodium**
**Exchanges: 3 meat, 2 starch, 3 vegetable**

# Broccoli Quiche

I like to make this when I have leftover mashed potatoes.

Vegetable oil cooking spray

2 cups mashed potatoes

8-ounce package Sargento Light
   reduced-fat shredded cheddar
   cheese

10-ounce package frozen chopped
   broccoli

1 onion, peeled and chopped

2 cloves garlic, peeled and minced
   (bottled is fine)

8 ounces egg substitute

1 cup skim milk

Preheat oven to 375°. Spray a 9-inch pie plate or quiche dish with cooking spray. Spread the mashed potatoes into the plate to form a crust and spray the top with cooking spray. Bake for 45 minutes. Into the prepared mashed potato crust, place the shredded cheese, broccoli, onion, and garlic. Mix together the egg and milk and pour over the vegetables. Bake for 40 minutes, increasing cooking time by 10 minutes if the quiche was made ahead of time and stored in the refrigerator.

**Makes 4 servings**
**Per serving: 306 calories, 29g protein, 30g carbohydrate, 10g fat,**
**22mg cholesterol, 572mg sodium**
**Exchanges: 3 meat, 1 starch, 1 1/2 vegetable**

There are days when it's easier to spend 10 minutes in the morning throwing ingredients together in the Crockpot and come home in the evening to a delicious meal all ready to serve.

# Chicken Cacciatore

I like to serve this over noodles and with a green salad.

1 pound boneless and skinless chicken tenders

28-ounce can crushed tomatoes

1 pound mushrooms, sliced

2 green bell peppers, cored and sliced

1 large onion, peeled and sliced

4 cloves garlic, peeled and minced (bottled is fine)

1 bay leaf

1 teaspoon crushed oregano

1 teaspoon dried basil

Salt to taste

Freshly ground black pepper to taste

6-ounce can tomato paste if needed

Place all ingredients except tomato paste in the Crockpot, cover, and cook on low for 8 to 10 hours. Add tomato paste if needed to thicken. Remove the bay leaf before serving.

**Makes 4 servings**
**Per serving: 250 calories, 32g protein, 23g carbohydrate, 4g fat,**
**69mg cholesterol, 517mg sodium**
**Exchanges: 3 meat, 4 vegetable**

# Beef Stew

This is a whole meal in one pot. It's one of my family's favorites.

1 pound lean stew beef

1 pound baby carrots

4 medium red potatoes, diced

4 stalks celery, diced

1 onion, peeled and diced

10.75-ounce can reduced-fat
tomato soup

1 cup red wine or cooking wine

4 cloves garlic, peeled and minced
(bottled is fine)

1 bay leaf

4 cloves

Salt to taste

Freshly ground black pepper to taste

10-ounce package frozen peas

Place all ingredients except peas in the Crockpot. Cover, and cook on low for 8 to 10 hours. Stir in peas. Remove bay leaf before serving.

Makes 4 servings
Per serving: 573 calories, 32g protein, 67g carbohydrate, 12g fat,
76mg cholesterol, 427mg sodium
Exchanges: 3 meat, 3 starch, 2 1/2 vegetable, 1 fat

# Jambalaya

I like to serve this with rice.

8 ounces boneless and skinless
chicken tenders

7 ounces Healthy Choice polska
kielbasa, sliced

28-ounce can stewed tomatoes

1 large onion, peeled and chopped

1 green bell pepper, cored and
chopped

1 red bell pepper, cored and
chopped

6 stalks celery, chopped

4 cloves garlic, peeled and
minced (bottled is fine)

1 teaspoon crushed thyme

1 teaspoon crushed oregano

Cayenne pepper to taste

10-ounce package frozen sliced okra

6-ounce can tomato paste, if needed

Place all ingredients except okra and tomato paste in the Crockpot. Cover, and cook on low for 8 to 10 hours. Stir in okra and add tomato paste if needed to thicken.

Makes 4 servings
Per serving: 226 calories, 24g protein, 26g carbohydrate, 3g fat,
57mg cholesterol, 885mg sodium
Exchanges: 3 meat, 4 vegetable

# Chicken Marsala

I like to serve this over noodles and with a green salad.

1 pound boneless and skinless chicken tenders

1 pound carrots, peeled and chopped

6 stalks celery, chopped

1 onion, peeled and chopped

1 pound mushrooms, sliced

1 cup marsala wine or cooking wine

4 cloves garlic, peeled and minced (bottled is fine)

1 bay leaf

Salt to taste

Freshly ground black pepper to taste

6-ounce can tomato paste if needed

Place all ingredients except tomato paste in the Crockpot. Cover, and cook on low for 8 to 10 hours. Add tomato paste if needed to thicken. Remove bay leaf before serving.

**Makes 4 servings**
**Per serving: 248 calories, 30g protein, 14g carbohydrate, 5g fat,**
**69mg cholesterol, 145mg sodium**
**Exchanges: 3 meat, 3 vegetable**

# Curried Chicken

I like to serve this over rice.

1 pound boneless and skinless chicken tenders

1 large onion, peeled and chopped

1 green bell pepper, cored and chopped

6 stalks celery, chopped

1 apple, cored and chopped

1 banana, peeled and chopped

1 cup chicken broth

2 cloves garlic, peeled and minced (bottled is fine)

2 tablespoons curry powder

1 bay leaf

Salt to taste

Freshly ground black pepper to taste

1/2 cup light coconut milk or skim milk

Place all ingredients except milk in the Crockpot. Cover, and cook on low for 8 to 10 hours. Stir in the milk. Remove bay leaf before serving.

**Makes 4 servings**
**Per serving: 232 calories, 29g protein, 20g carbohydrate, 4g fat,**
**70mg cholesterol, 324mg sodium**
**Exchanges: 3 meat, 1 vegetable, 1 fruit**

You may be wondering what desserts are doing in a healthy cookbook. Well, my family and I like desserts. I'm guessing that your family does too. These desserts are fruit- or dairy-based, so in addition to tasting good they also contribute to a healthy diet. I am offering two groups of desserts. The first group is desserts that are quick and easy to make but take longer than 5 minutes. I usually prepare these for company. The desserts in the second group are extremely simple and only take a few minutes to prepare. They are really ideas rather than recipes and they're a nice way to end your weeknight meals.

# Berry Trifle

Any combination of cake, pudding, and fruit will work well. The dessert looks beautiful when served in a trifle dish, but any glass bowl will work. This is an excellent make-ahead dessert, good for a crowd.

12-ounce prepared angel food cake

2 3.4-ounce packages instant
   fat-free vanilla pudding mix

4 cups skim milk

2 16-ounce packages frozen mixed
   unsweetened berries, thawed

12-ounce container Cool Whip Free

Cut or tear the angel food cake into 1-inch cubes. In a large bowl mix together the pudding mix and milk. Place half of the cake cubes in the bottom of a trifle dish or large glass bowl. Spread half of the pudding over the cake cubes. Place 1 package of mixed berries over the pudding. Top with half of the Cool Whip. Repeat the layers, garnishing the top with a few berries. Chill before serving.

**Makes 24 small servings**
**Per serving: 180 calories, 2g protein, 26g carbohydrate, 6g fat,**
**0 cholesterol, 230mg sodium**
**Exchanges: 1 starch, 1 fruit, 1 fat**

# Fruit Tart

Here is another excellent make-ahead dessert.
I am always asked for the recipe when I serve this.

6-ounce prepared reduced-fat
  graham cracker crust

8-ounce tub fat-free cream cheese
  with strawberries

4 cups various sliced fruit
  (strawberries, kiwi, mango,
  pineapple, etc.)

1/4 cup apricot or strawberry
  preserves

1 teaspoon lemon juice

Spread the cream cheese evenly on the piecrust. Arrange the sliced fruits attractively on top of the cream cheese. Heat the preserves in the microwave on high for about 30 seconds. Mix the preserves with the lemon juice and spread carefully on the fruit. Chill before serving.

**Makes 8 servings**
**Per serving: 156 calories, 6g protein, 31g carbohydrate, 2g fat,**
**2mg cholesterol, 303mg sodium**
**Exchanges: 1 starch, 1 fruit**

# Broiled Bananas

You can use rum in place of the lemon juice for a more sophisticated taste. I usually just use lemon juice. The warm bananas are also good topped with a scoop of fat-free vanilla frozen yogurt. This is an easy last minute dessert.

4 bananas, peeled and sliced thin

2 tablespoons brown sugar

1 tablespoon lemon juice

Preheat the broiler. Mix the bananas, sugar, and lemon juice together in a shallow baking pan or pie plate. Place under the broiler for a few minutes until the sugar melts and the bananas start to brown.

**Makes 4 servings**
**Per serving: 132 calories, 1g protein, 34g carbohydrate, 1g fat,**
**0 cholesterol, 4mg sodium**
**Exchanges: 2 fruit**

# Baked Apples

The warm apples are good topped with a scoop of fat-free vanilla frozen yogurt.

4 apples, peeled and cored

1/4 cup packed brown sugar

1 tablespoon lemon juice

1 teaspoon cinnamon

1/2 cup raisins

Preheat the oven to 375°. Place the apples in a shallow baking pan. Mix the remaining ingredients together and spoon over the apples. Bake, uncovered, for about an hour or until the apples are tender but not mushy.

**Makes 4 servings**
**Per serving: 180 calories, 1g protein, 47g carbohydrate, 0 fat,**
**0 cholesterol, 8mg sodium**
**Exchanges: 3 fruit**

# Fruit and Yogurt Parfait

This is another easy make-ahead dessert. It looks very attractive served in a glass wine goblet.

4 cups various sliced fruit
  (strawberries, kiwi, mango,
  pineapple, etc.)

16 ounces fat-free vanilla or
  lemon yogurt

1/2 cup wheat germ

In each of 4 large glass wine goblets, place a layer of fruit, yogurt, and wheat germ. Repeat the layers. Chill before serving.

**Makes 4 servings**
**Per serving: 201 calories, 10g protein, 39g carbohydrate, 2g fat,**
**0 cholesterol, 65mg sodium**
**Exchanges: 1 1/2 fruit, 1 milk**

# Apple Crisp

Another warm dessert that benefits from a scoop of fat-free vanilla frozen yogurt.

5 apples, peeled, cored, and sliced
  thin

1/3 cup sugar

1 teaspoon lemon juice

2 teaspoons cinnamon, divided

1 cup rolled oats

1/4 cup all-purpose flour

1/3 cup packed brown sugar

3 tablespoons melted butter or
  margarine

Preheat the oven to 375°. In a shallow baking dish or pie plate, combine the apples, sugar, lemon juice, and 1 teaspoon cinnamon. In a small bowl combine the oats, flour, brown sugar, butter or margarine, and remaining teaspoon cinnamon. Sprinkle the oat mixture over the apples. Bake, uncovered, for 40 to 45 minutes. Serve warm.

**Makes 8 servings**
**Per serving: 204 calories, 2g protein, 39g carbohydrate, 5g fat,**
**12mg cholesterol, 51mg sodium**
**Exchanges: 1 starch, 1 fruit, 1 fat**

# Weeknight Desserts

◆ Sliced bananas or grapes topped with a dollop of fat-free sour cream and a sprinkle of orange juice.

◆ Sliced bananas or apples drizzled with maple syrup and sprinkled with cinnamon or ground ginger.

◆ Orange or kiwi slices topped with fat-free vanilla yogurt.

◆ Melon or pineapple chunks drizzled with honey and sprinkled with dried mint.

◆ Berries topped with fat-free lemon yogurt.

◆ Canned fruit topped with reduced-fat granola cereal.

◆ Mixed dried fruit sprinkled with lemon juice and water, heated in the microwave.

◆ Applesauce sprinkled with cinnamon.

◆ Sherbet or sorbet with shortbread cookies.

◆ Fat-free vanilla frozen yogurt drizzled with chocolate syrup or topped with crushed gingersnap cookies.

◆ Sliced angel food cake topped with fat-free vanilla frozen yogurt and fruit.

◆ Ready-made fat-free pudding or jello.